Costantino D'Orazio

The keys to open 99 Secret places in Rome

Illustrations by
Danièle Ohnheiser

Translation by
Michael Macdonald

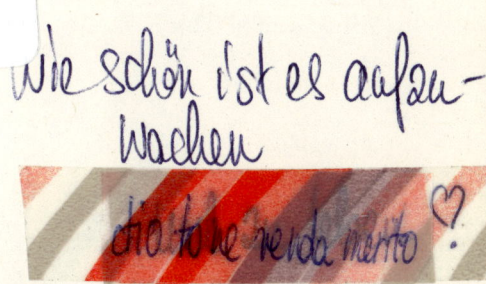

PALOMBI EDITORI

© April 2011
First Reprint August 2014
All rights reserved
Palombi & Partner Srl
via Gregorio VII, 224
00165 Roma

© 2017
Second Reprint May 2017
All rights reserved
Diano Libri Srl
Via Pietro Giardini, 186 - 41124 Modena

www.palombieditori.it

Layout, graphics
and editorial assistance
care of the publishing house

ISBN 978-88-6060-634-1

Contents

Foreword — 6

Palaces, houses, villas — 7

Convents, churches, libraries — 109

Underground places, mithraea, necropoles — 159

A gymnasium — 235

Cultural associations — 239

Index of places in order of appearance — 241

Index of places in alphabetical order — 245

Index of places by area — 249

Useful tips for the reader
Discovering extraordinary jewels and going beyond of the language barrier

This book is not a normal guide, but a collection of extraordinary places usually closed to the public. For the very first time everybody will find the information for a visit, as the author acquired them in a over fifteen-year work.
Usually a guide shows all the sites that you can see when you reach a city: this book works exactly in the opposite way. You will discover 99 jewels that usually nobody can see and you will also get the information to organize your own visit. The closed palaces, secret worship places and exclusive underground sites of Rome are much more than 99: this is a selection of the best ones that you can visit through special permits. In order to open their doors, you don't have to be "a friend of" and you don't need a peculiar reccomendation. Sometimes you just need some patience, because the private owners don't like to be bothered that much. No doubt, in this book you will get all the details and tools to reach the aim: discover treasure that so far has been available just for a happy few. Sometimes an email is enough, some other times you need to act with a bit of touch and diplomacy while you are asking for a visit. It might be useful to show up in a small group because sometimes the owners need to send a person just to open the site… and it may be difficult to do it just for a single visitor.
For the ones who don't speak Italian, it might be difficult to get in touch with the owners of these places. That's why at the end of the book you will find some of the best organizations that can help you in requesting the permits. It's their job: they can be your practical tool to get beyond the language barrier.
Even if the book has been conceived as a useful instrument, the author also told a lot of stories, anedocts and comments that offer new points of view about the Art of Rome. The description of the mithraea gives the chance to explain the contradictions of the God Mithra, who was very popular during the Roman Empire. While reading about the vaults of Palazzo Farnese, Palazzo Pamphilj and the Sistine Chapel, you will be able to understand the passage from Renaissance to Baroch. While entering the private palaces, like Palazzo Colonna and Palazzo Sacchetti, you will discover the stories of the amazing members of these families, who has managed to keep their commodities still in private hands after hundreds of years. This book gives you access to rooms where princes and countesses still live and preserve masterpieces commissioned by their ancestors. Some of the reasons why Rome attracts visitors from all over the world lay behind closed doors and inside residences where time has stopped, where the landlords still have the same names of the ones who lived two thousand years ago and where people are pride of being part of a great tradition.
The aim of this book is to shorten up impossible distances and offer the chance for experiencing places that you will never forget.

PALACES
HOUSES
VILLAS

1 Palazzo Colonna
where Princess Isabelle received Queen Elizabeth

For the visit
Piazza SS. Apostoli, 66
This is the address from which you may enter to visit Princess Isabelle's apartment, which is only opened for private booked viewings.
All you need to do is call 06 6784350,
send an e-mail to info@galleriacolonna.it, or go to www.galleriacolonna.it where you can find all the information you need. Guides are available for a fee.
Saturday morning the Colonna Gallery is open to the public, the entrance can be found at 17, via della Pilotta.

In one of the most majestic patrician palaces in the world, containing a gallery on a par with the great salons of Versailles, the Princes Colonna maintain the apartment that once belonged to Princess Isabelle exactly as it was when she was alive. Here it is possible to find the same cosy atmosphere, attention to detail, care to not move any of the family photos, next to the celebrated collection of thirty-seven scenes by Vanvitelli. Nor is it the only attraction to be found here in this place located on the ground floor of the palace which rises up from the foundations of the ancient Temple of Serapis. One of the few traces left of the old Roman sanctuary is the porphyry crocodile which greets visitors at the beginning of a sequence of rooms boasting various selected artists such as Pinturicchio, Pomarancio and the Cavalier Tempesta. The floor of the apartment is only in part that of the old "Venetian" style, seen in the Sala della Fontana; in all the other rooms the Princess had in fact changed the traditional coverings with a glossy oriental marble, perhaps inspired by her Lebanese origins.

The young daughter of Maronite bankers, Isabelle fell in love with Prince Marcantonio, who brought her to Italy, where she knew well how to make her mark on Roman society, at that time dealing with Mussolini's rise to power. «A great lady-in-waiting, intelligent, educated, conservative in the most pure and coherent sense, who after the fall of the monarchy found herself as a replacement to Maria José, as a "substitute Queen" hosting regal balls open only to crowned heads and from among the bourgeoisie only to financiers and bankers, provided that, obviously, they were not divorced» (as remembered by Laura Laurenzi in the daily newspaper la Repubblica on 18 November 1984, on the occasion of her funeral).

In the last few years of her life her apartment was transformed into an Aladdin's cave of treasures which she loved to show off only to her closest friends. On the wall, the canopy sporting the family crest can still be seen, in the centre of the rooms gilded wooden console are found on which depictions of chained Turks recall the famous battle of Lepanto in 1571, where Marcantonio Colonna halted the threat of the Muslim invasion. One of the rarest pieces is the painted night clock situated between two trunks in the old Sala della Fontana: inside a silent mechanism moves the numbers which are backlit by a candle. Shortly after, we find a strange double settee, called by the experts "confidence", bringing to mind the numerous encounters that must have been taking place here between these walls for over six hundred years.

In these rooms the presence of two other famous women from the family can still be felt: that of Maria Mancini, whose portrait by Simon Vouet is there, the latter being painter to the court of Louis XIV of France, and that of Olimpia Pamphilj, evoked by the doves and the olive branch painted on the ceilings of the first few rooms in the apartment. The first, niece of the powerful Cardinal Mazzarino, told in her diaries of the misadventures of her unhappy relationship with Lorenzo Onorio Colonna, from whom she ran away (*The chagrin of the Cardinal*, Sellerio Publishing). To have her return to Rome, he made sure that all the doors of the salons of Europe were closed to her. A sad end to a tale that started under the most favourable of circumstances, as shown by the ceiling painted by Giacinto Gimignani, which bears witness to the meeting between an antique column and a pair of fish, the heraldic symbol of the Mancini family. But even for a certain while Lorenzo Onorio and Maria must have been happy: Maratta and Dughet went so far as to paint their portrait in which they are depicted as Venus and Paris, just as perhaps they often appeared at their famous masquerade balls they loved to organize. On the walls next to their portrait in costume are nine fantastic small landscapes by Jan Bruegel the Elder, painted on copper to bring out the warmth of the reds and the crystalline splendor of the blues. Just one of the many hidden treasures in this dwelling which just goes to show how often it is possible to live tranquilly alongside such great works of art.

2 Casino Ludovisi
where Caravaggio got naked

For the visit
Via Lombardia, 46
The house is the property of Prince Niccolò Boncompagni Ludovisi, who receives visitors usually on a Friday or a Saturday morning.
To arrange a visit all you need do is call 06 483942.
If you are on your own it is possible for you to attach yourself to an existing group, groups can arrange visits.
Own Guide. Entrance fee.

Who knows in what state of mind Cardinal Francesco Maria Del Monte carried out his experiments in alchemy in the small room set up in his villa at Porta Pinciana, near Villa Medici. A certain awe must have come over him with the wall painting which he commissioned Caravaggio to paint in 1597 who had come up with the diabolical idea of doing his self portrait not just once but three times in the semblance of the supreme beings of the cosmos: Pluto, god of the underworld, Neptune, god of the Seas, Jupiter, god of everything else above ground. The artist, undertaking the first mural he had ever done (not as a fresco but with oils!), «feeling at fault for understanding neither the planes nor the prospective, so much so that he helped himself by placing the bodies seen from below on up, as he wanted to contrast the more difficult senses» (Bellori, 1672). He confronted this work as a new challenge where he would have to show his most daring mastery of foreshortening, a direct reference to the giant paintings by Giulio Romano in the Palazzo Te at Mantova. The dimensions of this room, even today being a passing point between two rooms, are so small as to ensure a sense of vertigo.

Neptune is shown embracing a horse of the sea with palm-like hooves, Jupiter is riding an eagle and Pluto, the most vigorous of the bunch, is standing on the clouds protected by a rather unintimidating Cerberus. It was the meekness of the dog that caused one person to draw similarities between it and the portrait of Cornacchia, the black poodle whom Caravaggio taught celebrated acrobatic numbers (Vodret). In the painting of the otherworldly entity the "damned" painter chose to proceed in a rather odd manner: you can see in it, above all, his genitals which must have been based on the artist's own, thanks to a mirror attached to the scaffolding. Once again proof of the extraordinary pragmatism of the Merisi. Try it and see…

It would have been something between irony and irreverence that

caused the painter to give his own face to the three divinities, metaphors for the three elements (earth, water and fire) which the Cardinal used to transform in his laboratory thanks to the potions contained in the alembics that can still be seen arranged in the niches along the walls. In 1597, the barber Pietropaolo gave to the police an unmistakable portrait of Caravaggio: «This painter is a hulking youngster of twenty or twenty five years with a short black beard, chubby, with thick eyelashes and black eyes, who goes around dressed in black rather shabbily, wearing a pair of ripped black stockings with long hair to his front». An identikit that leaves no room for error.

Capable of connecting in an inimitable way the most scurrilous and refined images, Caravaggio placed between the three divinities a wonderful celestial sphere within which four signs of the zodiac and two luminescent globes can be seen. A homage to Galileo Galilei with whom Cardinal del Monte had contacts, which was at that time disrespectful to the power of the Pope who deemed astronomical research a severe effrontery to the Church.

The recent discovery of this work has somewhat overshadowed the fame of another extraordinary painting, held in the main room of the house. It is a fresco of *Aurora* painted by Guercino in 1621 who had just arrived in Rome having been summoned by Cardinal Ludovico Ludovisi, who in the meantime had come into possession of the villa. Together with the *Fame*, which can be found in the room next to the alchemy room, the *Aurora* is one of the greatest works of the artist from Emilia, who must have surely fallen under the spell of the foreshortening invented by Caravaggio a few years before in the small room on the floor above. A heady, vertiginous architecture painted by the expert Agostino Tassi serves to draw the eye to a space that seems much higher than it is in reality, where a chariot that chases away the night passes. Just as the light engulfs the Earth and signals the break of day, the papacy of Gregory XV would have brought new prosperity to the Ludovisi. An omen which can be seen yet again in the fresco *Fame* on the floor above where Glory is accompanied by Honour, Virtue and *Amor Virtutis*.

3 Villa Albani
where you can admire original Greek and Etruscan frescoes

For the visit
Via Salaria, 92
Visits are allowed for small groups, received once a week, without a set schedule.
You need to send a fax to the Amministrazione Torlonia with your request (including the names and surnames of participants) to 06 68199934 or an e-mail to amministrazione@srdps.191.it.
For further information call 06 6861044.
Own guide. Free entrance.

It has always been considered one of the most inaccessible collections in the world. It is said that, to see it, the archaeologist Ranuccio Bianchi Bandinelli dressed up as the cleaner whose job it was to take out the rubbish. It is still not possible to see the entire collection of 620 statues conserved in the store rooms of the house on via della Lungara. But every so often Prince Torlonia allows small groups to visit the other extraordinary family collection at Villa Albani.

Discreetly and in a way compatible with everyday life of a private home, still lived in today, it is possible to admire some of the works in the world's most desirable collection.

Villa Albani hosts one of Rome's most refined parks, which protects the residence of Cardinal Alessandro Albani, nephew of Pope Clement XI. We are in the middle of the 18th century and the Cardinal decides to build a country house in an area that shortly afterwards will be subject to one of the main real estate speculations following the unification of Italy. Today the villa remains an oasis of tranquility and green in the heart of Rome a stone's throw away from Piazza Fiume, at the beginning of via Salaria, one of the city's busiest areas. To take a stroll in the park is to leave behind the urban chaos and step into a dimension where time stands still.

Perhaps it is the care that is taken with the bushes and trees creating a decorative garden adorned with statues and fountains, but few other town residences can boast the same refinement (Villa Tasca in Palermo, Villa Belpoggio in Bologna…). When the Torlonias acquired the property they also bought the collection put together by Cardinal Albani in the 1700s with the help of Winkelmann, one of the most notable historians of the time. He is the father of this taste for antiquity and inventor of the theories on neoclassical aesthetics through rereading the ancient works. He is also attributed with setting out the iconographic program followed by Anton Raphael Mengs which culminated in the creation of the *Parnassus* on the ceiling of the salon on the Villa's main floor. From amongst the most famous works in the collection a special place of honour must be reserved for the Etruscan frescoes from the tomb of Francois di Vulci (IV century B.C.), which can be admired close up as they are resting on an iron railing, or the *Antinous*, an extraordinary sculpture of Greek origin. In the collection we can find some of the European Masters' greatest works of art, from Perugino to Tintoretto, from Giulio Romano to Guercino, David, Ribera and Vanvitelli. All rigorously connected to this extraordinary setting: the only place where they can be discovered and admired.

4 Palazzo Farnese
where the baroque style painting was born

For the visit
Piazza Farnese, 67
The visits of the Palazzo are organized by the Association "Inventer Rome".
The visits are scheduled every Monday, Wednesday and Friday at 3pm, 4pm and 5pm also in English.
Reserve your visit through the email visite-farnese@inventerrome.com or visit the website www.inventerrome.com
Phone n. +393493683013.
Guides available.
Entrance fee.

Behind a Roman building you will usually find a Pope. Martin V for Palazzo Colonna, Clement X for Palazzo Altieri, Innocent X for Palazzo Pamphilj. Each time a building was the chosen instrument of propaganda for the Pope to show the world the heights to which his family had risen to. Art and architecture have always been in the service of "politics": one of the most striking examples is Palazzo Farnese. It was of such a size that its building started long before Cardinal Alessandro became Pope Paul III, the pope of the Council of Trento. Almost twenty years before being nominated Pope, he invited one of the most prolific architects of the age, Antonio da Sangallo the Younger to devise the reconstruction of a modest residence bought a few years before close to Campo de' Fiori, at that time the business centre of Rome. It seems that Sangallo initially laid down plans for a "Florentine" project, with a smooth façade and workshops on the ground floor. But when the elections came round, the building was transformed into an opulent factory, almost thirty metres high and sixty metres long (nicknamed the "the dice"): the courtyard is made up of two spans and the facade gives onto the piazza making this the Farnese family's location for celebrations, and imagine that the house even before that hosted a court of over 360 people!

In 1546 Sangallo died and the Pope called upon Michelangelo to continue the work. Between the two there was already a trusting relationship, as it was Paul III who, in 1534, had asked Buonarroti to paint the Last Judgment in the Sistine Chapel. And his choice of the Florentine genius did not disappoint. Michelangelo made essential modifications to the project, which even today are at the base of this building's majestic beauty. The first new addition is the lengthening of the façade's upper cornice, thus making the roof invisible from the piazza and outlining the building directly against the sky (a similar case can also be found on the project at Piazza del Campidoglio). It is his choice to place two antique columns to the sides of the central full-length window decorated with the enormous Farnese coat-of-arms, with the lilies of both Florence and France. But the detail which surprises the most was the idea to cover the building in differently coloured bricks in such a way as to create refined geometric patterns between the windows. Discovered only during the restorations in 2000, it is something that remains unique in Rome today.

If you cross the piazza at night and raise your eyes above the portal you may catch glimpses of the frescoes in the Sala dei Fasti Farnesiani. Today it houses the French Ambassador's office, who sometimes leaves the lights on so everyone can see the splendid masterpiece by Francesco Salviati and the Zuccari brothers. To discover the other famous treasure hidden in the building you must venture up to the first floor on the side which faces the second internal courtyard (which held at one time the famous statue of Hercules, now in Naples). We are talking about the Carracci Gallery, dedicated to the loves of the Gods. At the beginning it must have been a small "room" but the work grew and grew until it became the birthplace of baroque painting, under Hannibal Carracci with his brother Agostino and a stable of assistants, amongst whom was numbered Domenichino. From 1587, the Masters worked for about seven years on the decorations which artists from around the world would come to admire and to learn the new methods of painting after the ceiling in the Sistine Chapel.

Michelangelo's sculptural bodies in the hands of the Carracci brothers move freely in the air on this ceiling, they animate the space and create a vortex of emotions. This gallery "exceeded" the layout of the Sistine Chapel's ceiling thanks to the invention of a continuous sky which acts as a background to a series of paintings. They seem like canvases hanging on the wall, but they are in fact

frescoes: something completely new to Rome. It is the beginning of a new era, inaugurated here by the passions of *Jupiter and Juno, Diana and Endimion, Pan and Arianna, Polyphemus* and *Galatea,* up to the *Triumph of Bacchus and Arianna*, at the centre of the ceiling just as Ovid recounted in his Metamorphoses. The choice to decorate such an important subject with such a profane and not in the least prim subject (the Gods who surrender to love!) had a great effect on the contemporaries of the Counter-Reformation's Pope. But reference to the classical period runs throughout the whole of Palazzo Farnese, where now only the echo remains of the numerous sculptures that used to decorate the corners of the building. In the 18th century it all ended up in Naples, to where Carlo di Borbone, the last heir to the Farnese, transferred his court. The Palace, which in the 17th century had already played host to Cristina of Sweden and other French Ambassadors, gradually parted ways with the family's destiny. Sold in 1894 to France, it was ransomed by Mussolini who, in 1936 gave it again to the government in Paris for 99 years with payment of a symbolic rent (1 Lira a year). Only sixteen years remain until the end of the contract: What will Palazzo Farnese's destiny be after that?

> Until the end of April 2011 ordinary visits are suspended due to the exceptional exhibition which sees the return of the Farnese collection to Rome. To book a visit to the exhibition call 06 32810.

5 Palazzo Pamphilj
where Mrs. Pimpaccia fell in love with Pope Innocent X

For the visit
Piazza Navona, 14
The Brazilian Embassy has organized a very efficient booking service, but it is only via internet.
Therefore, anyone wanting to visit Palazzo Pamphilj must go at least one month before to www.ambasciatadelbrasile.it and follow the instructions found at the bottom of the homepage. For further information you can write to visitas@ambrasile.it or call 06 683981.
Visits take place every two weeks on a Tuesday. Own Guides. Free entrance.

Few women such as Olimpia Maidalchini have earned the worst nicknames ever to have been invented by the Romans. The "*Papessa*", the "*Pimpaccia*" (a play on words in Latin meaning once religious now full of sin), and other epithets too rude to mention here, were given to the woman, who in the 17th century dominated the town's political scene for almost fifteen years, alongside her brother-in-law, Giovan Battista Pamphilj, who was, thanks to her, elected Pope in 1644 as Innocence X.

Theirs was an ironclad alliance based on the enormous wealth of Lady Olimpia, earned through a prudent series of well-chosen marriages, and the noble prestige of the Pamphiljs, which the Lady managed to attain by marrying Pamphilio, thirty years her senior. The portrait by the sculptor Alessandro Algardi (held at the Doria Pamphilj Gallery) gives us the impression of a determined lady, but not beautiful by any stretch of the imagination. However, Olimpia made wise use of the artists of the day to transform Pope Innocence X's papacy into one of the most refined and prolific in history. Then, as today, jubilee years were important dates to be respected with stately public works. The one in 1650 was no exception and was celebrated with the utmost lavishness and glory thanks to some extraordinary architectural undertakings, concentrated for the most part in Piazza Navona, still decorated today with its Pamphilj doves. It seems that Borromini worked on the church of Sant'Agnese in Agone (practically the private chapel of Palazzo Pamphilj) only by managing to get into the Pimpaccia's good graces, thanks to father Virgilio Spada, the Pope's almsgiver and a rare intellectual. But, for the same reason, that is, in those years artists' careers depended so much on the fickle nature of the woman, the project for the central fountain in Piazza Navona ended up being taken away from Borromini and was then purloined by Bernini thanks to his cunning stratagem of making a silver miniature of his fountain and donating this as a surprise to the Pamphiljs, thrilling the Pope and pilfering the project from his rival. While the two most celebrated architects of the Baroque waste time spiting one another, a third artist, better-known as a painter, comes onto the scene as a main character in Palazzo Pamphilj and creates here one of his masterpieces, *Scenes from the life of Aeneas*. He is Pietro Berrettini da Cortona, already famous for his frescoes in the Sala Barberini on via delle Quatro Fontane, painted for Pope Urban VIII.

He will paint the gallery of the new residence in Piazza Navona, signaling the turning of a corner in modern painting.

To simplify and clarify somewhat the history of art at that time, we have to reflect on the transition from Renaissance painting to Baroque painting by analyzing three famous ceiling frescoes: the Sistine Chapel's by Michelangelo, that of the Gallery at Palazzo Farnese, masterpiece of Hannibal Carracci and the ceiling in the Aeneas room, painted by Cortona in 1651 in Palazzo Pamphilj. The presence of painted architecture, which in the Sistine Chapel constitutes the supporting structure for the entire pictorial cycle, gradually disappears to leave the space to a continuous flux of human figures and stories taking place above our heads uninterruptedly. It is this challenge that Berrettini wins in the gallery in Piazza Navona, designed by Borromini, who leaves his mark with delicate natural decorations on the doors and windows. For the first time we find ourselves in an environment with only two Palladian style archway posted at the very end of the room. And this is the point of departure for the Cortona project, which takes into account the two opposing sources of light which give sense and direction to the narration. It begins on the side that faces onto the Piazza, where Juno beseeches Aeolus to unleash a storm against the fleet of Aeneas, hated by the Goddess for being the son of her rival, Venus. Turning our back to the window, the events surrounding the mythical founder of the Roman people unfold who, with the help of the Gods, of the Sibyl Cumana and above all the admirable council of his father, Anchises, manages to overcome innumerable misfortunes to finally reach the Italic coast and found a new colony. Not, however, without having first provoked Jupiter's intervention, who placates his consort's anger towards the Trojans. We are in front of a new celebration of the origins of Rome, told through one of the most popular tales of the age, and well-known to the ambassadors and nobility alike who crossed the palace's threshold. Today the Gallery still concludes an extraordinary journey passing through seven rooms, alternating biblical and classical themes with paintings by some of the most active artists in 17th-century Rome. Giacinto Gimignani worked in the Sala di Giuseppe and perhaps also in the Moses Room. The Sala delle Tempeste (the Storms Room) is by Agostino Tassi, more famous for the scandalous rape of Artemisia Gentileschi. Gaspa Dughet, an expert landscape artist, painted the Sala dei Paesi, where he reached one of the heights of his career. A fascinating tour, which starts from a huge salon, obtained by closing a loggia, which the Roman Philharmonic Society, when it had its home here, dedicated to the composer Pier Luigi da Palestrina.

6 Palazzo Sacchetti
where architect Sangallo was neighbour to Raphael

For the visit
Via Giulia, 66
To visit the palace it is advisable to go in groups of at least twenty. If this number is not reached the management requests you pay the price of a full group. To arrange a date and manner for your visit you can call 06 68308950 or send a fax to 06 6877079 or write an email to amm.sacchetti@alice.it
Own guide.
Entrance fee.

An inscription on the facade of Palazzo Sacchetti reminds us that the building belonged to the famous Florentine architect, Antonio da Sangallo the Younger, member of one of the most prolific artistic families of the Roman Renaissance.

They received the land directly from Pope Paul III Farnese for whom they were creating the family abode just a few metres away. Actually, the presence of Sangallo on this street was never a question of luck, since the failure of Pope Julius II's project the area had been transforming itself into the general quarter for the Florentine nobility in Rome, and the architect was one of the artists closest to the hearts of the Tuscan families. His is the initial project for the church of San Giovanni dei Fiorentini, right next door to the house. It seems that Raphael had settled at number 85 on this street, the first great artery in Rome to cut through the tight medieval passageways, because at that time the most important urban projects of the century were being carried out in that area. Via dei Tribunali (today via Giulia) was supposed to be close to the Tiber originally, but maybe it was exactly the close proximity to the river and its frequent flooding that discouraged Julius II's project and sank the plans of Bramante, to whom the Pope had turned.

If we can't be one hundred percent certain of Raphael's real property ownership, the fact that Sangallo was at Palazzo Sacchetti is backed up by many documents, and on the death of the architect in 1546 – having only worked on it for four years – it was sold to Cardinal Ricci di Montepulciano (another Tuscan).

It was only in 1649 that the building passed to the Sacchettis,

Florentine merchants and bankers, who still live there today. Over a period of one hundred and fifty years the rise of the family was continuous and progressive, thanks above all to the ability of Giovan Battista, who gained the title of marquis, and to Cardinal Giulio Sacchetti, who in the 17th century was confirmed in the Papal administration. Proof of his power was the acquisition of the Palazzo

and the building of the family chapel inside the church of San Giovanni, which was passed to Lanfranco in 1615. There were few changes made by the Sacchetti to the building, which had already been completed by Cardinal Ricci.

The enlargement of the building was the work of Nanni di Baccio Bigio, a pupil of Sangallo's, while the decoration on the main floor, today known as the Salone dei Mappimundi (Room of World Maps) is the work of Francesco Salviati.

After crossing the courtyard, you go up a dark staircase which takes you to a series of corridors and rooms where finally you reach the room where they still have on show the canopy which at one time was kept behind the throne used by the Pope when papal hearings were held in the building.

Hanging in the Sala da Pranzo (Lunch Room) are two remarkable paintings by Pietro da Cortona (*Sacra Famiglia* and *Adam and Eve*), the only surviving paintings from over twenty works by the artist, along with a collection of almost 700 pieces gathered by the family and today dispersed all over the world. Maybe it was due, amongst others, to the fact that none of the able Cardinals in the family ever became Pope that the Sacchetti suffered a serious financial crisis in the 18th century forcing them to forego many of their properties, with the exception of the property on via Giulia.

On the main floor we have the cavernous Salone dei Mappamondi where il Salviati created frescoes of some of the stories of David: from the encounter with Saul, to Bathsheba at her Bath and David's dance at his haranguing of the soldiers.

We are faced with the triumph of Mannerism, liberated from the rules and proportions of the Renaissance, free to experiment with new balances as demonstrated by the careful and innovative arrangement of the scenes between freely set out cornices on the room's imposing walls.

At one time the building looked directly onto the Tiber and was sign posted for those who arrived by river by a rather unusual warning, still visible today to those travelling along the Lungotevere: two ancient theatre masks and a bust of Juno standing on the roof of a small lodge built in the palace's garden. More than a simple decoration, a serious invitation to give it a wide berth.

7 Palazzo dei Penitenzieri
where Pinturicchio painted a mysterious ceiling

For the visit
Via della Conciliazione, 33
Visiting the rooms of the Ordine Equestre del Santo Sepulcro (the Equestrian Order of the Holy Sepulchre) – not to be confused with the wing of the Hotel Columbus – is possible from Monday to Friday after 14:30.
To arrange the day and method of your visit you need to call 06 6828121 or send a fax to 06 68802298 or an e-mail to gmag@oessh.va.
Own guide.
A contribution is appreciated.

For the pilgrims who came to Rome in search of absolution, even the basilica at St. Peter's was not without its hidden dangers. Foreigners, for example, had often to ask for the help of an interpreter in order to say confession not knowing that their generous helpers would then demand to be paid to keep their secrets of the confessional. To cut out this widespread practice, in 1338, Pope Benedict XII brought into being the Penitentiary Brotherhood whose job was to oversee the confessional and provide assistance to the sadly misunderstood pilgrims. To these in the 17th century Pope Alexander VII entrusted the building that Cardinal Francesco della Rovere had commissioned to Baccio Pontelli in the Rione district two centuries earlier. At the time it gave onto Piazza Scossacavalli, which disappeared with the opening of via della Conciliazione. The building imitates the structure of Palazzo Venezia. Today it is equally divided between the Hotel Columbus and the Equestrian Order of the Holy Sepulchre, who bought it in 1943 to transform it into their headquarters.

It is here they open the doors to the salons with completely frescoed walls from the time of Cardinal della Rovere, who decides to dedicate the rooms of his dwelling to typical subjects of the Humanist culture at a time when the subjects of Greco-roman classicism undergo the most daring interpretations in a religious sense.

It was in the 15th century that Neo-Platonism, a philosophy that tried to reconcile the most rational logic with faith in Christian dogma, came back into fashion. Art was one of the most efficient vehicles for this new mentality which offered a useful key to reading the complicated frescoes in the Palazzo dei Penitenziari. In the first room only traces remain of the trompe-l'oeil architecture where no signs remain of the landscapes that would maybe once have adorned them.

In the next room we can still spot remnants of some representations of the months, shown through activities in fields and crowned with their corresponding zodiacal signs. It is the first nod towards an attempt to forge a connection between the destiny of man and the power of the stars, which in Italy can be found in many other *palazzi* (the most famous being Palazzo Schifanoia in Ferrara). Thus the month of November hosts the mythological affair of Orion, who is bitten by a scorpion sent by Diana against mankind as a punishment. Moved to pity, Zeus transforms both the animal and the hunter into constellations, placing them to the antipodes of the heavenly skies. A small example to clarify that in the past there was not a clear distinction between pagan culture and religious culture, nor was there a clear borderline between science and superstition. It could be for this reason that we today find it so difficult to interpret the ceiling painted by Pinturicchio in the last room of the Palace, called that of the "demi-gods". The artist commissioned sixty three octagonal wooden panels laid out in ordered rows to cover the entire surface. Instead of painting directly on to the panels, he decided to operate in tempera on sheets of paper which he would then stick onto the wood. The explanation for this unusual technique lies possibly in the choice of subjects he painted. These "demi-gods" are nothing more than mythological creatures with half human, half animal bodies, taken for the most part from medieval bestiaries or accounts of exotic cultures. Two-headed sirens, sphinxes, tritons, dolphins held by putti and centaurs ready for battle. To create the smallest details, often invisible from below, Pinturicchio made use of a technique very similar to miniature painting which he had learned as a boy. And it is from this repertoire of miniature books that such enigmatic characters emerge. In each runs a theme of red that contrasts with the fake gilded mosaic background. What we have here apparently are not very well specified call for morality and prudence, where the artist had fun devising the most eccentric iconographies. Fortune, for example, is a winged creature riding a dolphin. In her hands she holds a sail, full with wind being blown by the movement of the fish. A small movement is sufficient to make it turn!

8 Palazzo Falconieri
where Borromini left his esoteric testament

For the visit
Via Giulia, 1
Since 1928 Palazzo Falconieri has been the seat of the Hungarian Academy who permit booked visits by individuals and groups. Call 06 6889671 or send a fax to 06 68805292 or an e-mail to: accademiadungheriain roma4@tin.it.
Own guide.
Entrance fee.

Maybe it was here at Palazzo Falconieri that Borromini felt more free than ever to try something that no one had dared do before: intertwine esoteric and mysterious symbols which certainly had nothing to do with classical or religious iconography.

Probably thanks to the closely shared views of Orazio Falconieri, who commissioned the works, the artist was able to create the decorations for four of the rooms on the first floor of the building, which still today, depict hard to interpret representations. You have to refer to a Masonic repertoire and to the combination of elements coming from the Orient and relating to alchemy to understand what the owners of this house wanted to represent with these stuccoes. Following a completely random order, we can start from the ceiling where three crowns of intertwined laurel are crossed with the rays of a smiling sun set in the centre. There are three circles and three rays of light: a number which brings together both the Christian Holy Trinity and the Cabala. The sun could represent a sign of vital energy, which seems to have had its effect on the swirls of plants which flower vigorously and infinitely over the entire surface. Looking closely, Borromini has hidden amongst the plants tiny birds, insects and exotic animals. The architect worked here with the same ability as a painter, modeling the stucco with sprightly genius to define the smallest of details.

The decoration in the next room would seem to have a more political air about it. The ceiling here is dominated by an oval which contains a globe placed on the floor. The sphere, crossed by meridians and parallels, is also crossed by a snake biting its tail (*Uroboros*), in its turn held by a crown of laurel and marked with a scepter. On the far side there is an eye issuing rays of light, to the other the globe. It isn't hard to realize that we are here in front of a complex and articulated celebration of Power which will gloriously govern the Earth forever. Is it the power of the Falconieris? Borromini does not explain to which source the eye refers, to God or to the Masons. However, this ambiguity may not be unintentional. More enlightening and clear is evocation of the family in the falcon which is represented in four stages, alighting on a festoon and then agilely taking flight again. In the corners we find the symbol of the Scaglieri, to whom the Falconieri were connected, and the cornucopia, omen of prosperity. The meaning of these decorations is not the only enigma hidden inside the Falconieri Palace. The use of space here is not entirely clear either. The rooms with the most prestigious décor can be found in a side wing of the building, but they aren't of a size to indicate use for audiences. Perhaps they were used for special guests at confidential meetings who must have experienced a certain fascination. Perhaps it was right here that the Falconieri signed their contracts which enabled them to accumulate vast fortunes thanks to the right to collect tax on salt. It is thanks to their financial acumen that they were welcomed in Rome by Pope Paul III and managed to acquire a mansion on via Giulia becoming one of the most important Florentine families on the scene in Rome. Such was their desire for oneupmanship that they invited Borromini to work out a system to elevate their building to a point even higher than Palazzo Farnese. The architect from Ticino came up with one of his most successful tricks and placed on top of Palazzo Falconieri a majestic turret up which you can still climb today and enjoy one of the most incredible views of Rome. A short walk from the Pantheon, it seems as if you could jump to the rooftop of Palazzo Farnese, were it not for the two-faced busts set on an elegant balustrade, that is as refined as it is innocuous.

9 Palazzo della Cancelleria

where you will find an underground lake

For the visit
Piazza della Cancelleria, 1
The palace can be visited, by booking only, on Tuesdays and Saturdays.
You need to contact the Amministrazione del Patrimonio della Sede Apostolica on 06 69893405 or to sent email to economato@apsa.va.
Own guide.
Entrance fee.

Entering the Main Hall on the first floor of Palazzo della Cancelleria inspires a certain reverential awe. Perhaps because this is the place where the Sacra Rota still meet today, with its wooden benches for the court and its entourage, laid out as if at any moment the trial will begin. It is the largest room in the building, with frescoes from the 18th century in dark tones and irregular lighting. Here, under the clock painted by Baciccia, famous sessions have taken place, as that of the tragic year of 1848, which led to the brief Roman Republic. In fact in the 16th century this enormous room was used originally as an ante camera to the apartment used by Cardinal Raphael Riario, great-grandson of Pope Sixtus IV, who in 1483 was given by his uncle the title of San Lorenzo in Damaso. Thanks to which privilege, as was his by right at that time, he became chancellor, one of the most influential roles in the Papal court. The Cardinal had the role of drawing up, writing and enacting papal measures: he was trusted with the refining of the laws and their definitive wording (today many of these tasks are carried out by the Secretary of State). An ambitious man with an exuberant character, Cardinal Riario decided that with his arrival the Chancellery would have to be transformed into a majestic residence worthy of the "second office of the State".

He was the one who paved the way for the work that would give to Rome one of its first Renaissance palaces, inspired by the Greco-Roman aesthetic. It is the beginning of a new era for the city, the debut of a new architectural style which looks to the works of Leon Battisti Alberti in Florence and uses the materials that Rome has to offer, such as marble, which for this building seems to have also come from the nearby Teatro di Pompeo. One of the artists who had some of the responsibilities for the Palazzo della Cancelleria project was undoubtedly Bramante, to whom the design of the grand courtyard has been attributed. A perfect construction on three levels, supported by beautiful ancient columns. In reality, there is no documentation to attest to the fact he worked there, just as we cannot be sure that Andrea Bregno worked on the façade, but the Palace is certainly one of the clearest signs of the new tastes that were making their way onto the scene in Rome. It has an enormous smooth ashlar façade which protrudes just a little, rows of architrave windows, antique-style balustrades and, most of all, a very regular rhythm between full and empty. Something similar had only been seen in Rome at Palazzo Venezia. We are now in the '80s of the 15th century: a group of extraordinary painters are about to decorate the walls of the Sistine Chapel and many more architects are called upon to redesign the "face" of the city which over the course of a century would abandon its medieval look and become the heart for innovative artistic flair, taking away first place from Venice and Florence. An enterprising personality such as Riario was needed to step on the accelerator and bring about this revolution. Incredible stories were already at that time circulating about him, such as his having won 14,000 ducats (at least three million euro in today's money)at the expense of Franceschetto Cybo, son of Cardinal Giovanni Battista Cybo, the future Pope Innocence VIII. It was apparently thanks to this sum that Riario was able to have work started on the enlargement of his property. In addition to a great architect (whose identity is not yet certain), the artists involved in the decoration of the interior (Vasari, Salviati, Perin del Vaga) were amongst the most interesting ones of the 16th century, the century in which the palace passed to Cardinal Alessandro Farnese, vice-chancellor of Pope Paul III, his uncle. It is to him that the most beautiful room is dedicated, known as the "Room of a Hundred Days". Soon he would engage Giorgio Vasari to complete the fresco which tells the story of the main events from the Farnese papacy. It is said that the painter boasted to Michelangelo about his work, and the only response from the latter was to ironically state, «you can tell!»! It was actually Vasari himself who complained of having had to employ a large number of coworkers in order to meet the strict deadlines imposed on him by the patron. It is still extraordinary, however, to see such an invention as the grand staircases rising from the floor and almost inviting the observer to go up inside the painting to the level of the figures which are moving around within an architecture of Solomonic columns (one century before Bernini put them around the altar at St. Peter's).

Vasari's masterpiece is one of the most representative proofs of Mannerism, a language in which he knew how to express himself with sophistication even on much smaller surfaces, such as those painted by Francesco Salviati in the private chapel of Palazzo della Cancelleria, dedicated to St. Paul (the Pope's namesake), and Perin del Vaga's extraordinary scenes from the Bible in another room on the main floor.

Amongst the buildings most amazing secrets we must include the Sepulchre of Aulo Irzio, found purely by chance in 1938 underneath the building. Its tuff enclosure is completely submerged in the clear waters of the Euripus, a canal that used to cross Campo Marzio to eventually flow into the Tiber. During work on the levees at the end of the 19th century the canal became blocked, causing the water level to rise and consequently flood the surrounding area. This site bore the brunt of it, but today it seems even more mysterious and fascinating, at the end of a journey which from the Renaissance goes back to the 1st century A.D., underground and… underwater.

10 Aurora Pallavicini's Casino
where the ceiling is reflected in a mirror

For the visit
Via XXIV Maggio, 43
Bookings for visits cannot be made over two weeks in advance. You need to call 06 4814344 or write an e-mail to: aurorapallavicini@saita.it. Guides are available. Entrance fee.

It is rare for a patrician palace today still to belong to the same family who built it hundreds of years ago. Excluding rare cases, such as Palazzo Colonna and Palazzo Odescalchi, almost all the others have changed hands at one time or another and, as always happens, underwent transformation upon the arrival of each new owner. This is also the case with Palazzo Pallavicini-Rospigliosi which was, in actual fact, the idea of one Cardinal Scipione Borghese at the beginning of the 17th century. It was he who commissioned Giovanni Vasanzio to construct a garden on three levels, the highest part of which is reserved for the Casino dell'Aurora. A corner of tranquility and meditation, despite its being only a few metres from Piazza del Quirinale with all its traffic and daily hordes of tourists. After the Borgheses, who made use of the foundations of the Baths of Constantine, the building passed on to the Altemps, to the Bentivoglios, to the Lantes, to Cardinal Mazzarino and to his heirs, the Mancinis. It was the latter who ceded it to the Pallavicini-Rospiglisi, a line passing through many complex family affairs which sees this double-barreled name split and reform many times. They hold, however, the record for the longest ownership of the property: over three hundred years, since 1704. Of the many important Pallavicinis, the memory in Rome of Princess Elvina, who passed away in 2004, is still fresh.

A strong and feisty character, Donna Elvina for years made the Palace on the Quirinale a meaningful reference point not only for all the Roman nobility, but also for the Vatican and the political world. Her views on matters, often controversial and against the current, have always constituted a decisive front which the city had to match. The arrival on the Quirinale of some very special paintings enriching the already important collection here is entirely thanks to her: amongst its masterpieces Botticelli's *La Derilitta*, Rubens' *Twelve Apostles* and a portrait by Van Dyck, held in the private apartment on the first floor of the building (these cannot be visited). Only a small portion of these treasures is on exhibition in the Casino. We can admire here Luca Giordano's *Julian the Apostate* and the *Conversion of Saul*, Guido Reni's *Andromeda* and a stunning Crucifix, work carried out by the Emilian master in the 1640's. Thirty years before, Reni actually worked at Palazzo Pallavicini, where he produced one of his finest works: the *Aurora's Chariot* which crosses the ceiling of the Casino. It is a carried picture, which means that the painter did not address the problem of a perspective from below and did not try to deceive the eye by pushing the image into infinity. Reni painted it as if he were painting on a canvas and because of this it is advisable to look at it with the mirror, available in the centre of the room, which restores the painting to its two-dimensional nature. Apollo's chariot rises from the sea on the left preceded by Aurora who is scattering flowers together with Phosphorous, the first star of the morning, represented by a winged putto. In a great effort for realism, the sun presents itself as a dazzling light behind Apollo, at the helm of his chariot. The greatest merit in this painting lies precisely in Guido Reni's capacity to recreate the effect of the morning light, when the sun illuminates the Earth from a precise point and on the other side of the sky darkness still prevails. The pink and orange of the day bring with them warmth which dispels the cold of the different blues. The hours move to the foreground, creating a dance of colours moved by the wind. On the outside of the Casino, on the façade, you can admire numerous antique bas-reliefs placed into the wall like paintings on a wall: a remarkable collection of mythological subjects ranging from Dionysus to Endymion, which constituted the "antique" section of the collection.

11 The Apartment of the Council of State at Palazzo Spada

where a statue witnessed Julius Caesar's murder

For the visit
Piazza Capodiferro, 13
The Superintendence office organizes a visit to the Palace, which also includes the apartment of the Council of State, every first Sunday of the month. To book call 06 6832409.
To visit just the apartment, you can contact the body directly which on Saturdays sometimes opens up the main floor to cultural association groups or individuals who can join an existing group. In this case you need to call 06 68272239 or send a fax to 06 68272238.
Entrance free.

The building is renowned for Borromini's celebrated perspective gallery, an extraordinary optical illusion which remains one of the most representative outcomes from the spirit of the Baroque, between scientific research and artifice. For those who don't know it, just think it is 8 metres long but seems to be 37 metres in depth thanks to the proportions and inclinations worked out in the planes devised by the architect to fool the spectator's gaze (to see it all you need do is go to the ticket office at the Galleria Spada which offers daily visits). Not many know, however, that on the main floor of Palazzo Spada the Cardinal's apartment still exists, occupied today by the Council of State. The bogeyman of many an administrative provision, the tribunal that defends the rights of the citizen against the Public Administration, is also the custodian of one of the most precious places in Rome, which has managed to conserve almost intact the fresco decoration and, above all, the stucco so rare in the Capital's residences. The layout of the rooms is due to the work of two of the most important characters in the history of the Palace, Cardinal Girolamo Capodiferro and Cardinal Bernardino Spada, brother of Virgilio who was friend and protector to so many artists in the 17th century. If the first one dedicated himself above all to the construction of the building and its external decoration, it was Spada starting in the 1730's, who rearranged the private apartment. Already at the entrance, one remains literally "rooted to the spot": the two sides of the corridor which runs around the courtyard hold some true rarities. In the gallery you can admire some bas-reliefs, set into the wall, whilst the ceiling hosts a meridian, useful for calculating the hour in different countries between the East and the West, from Spain to Mesopotamia. It is a reproduction of a plan created by Padre Emmanuel Maignan in the convent of the Trinità dei Monti (for more information see p. 111), which Virgilio Spada also wanted at his brother's house. Once again geometric precision goes arm in arm with visual wonder, because the intertwining of lines and symbols allows you to know the time over a vast geographic area. More immediate and stirring is the effect of the next gallery, where Giulio Mazzoli's Michelangelesque school created a series of stucco works framing paintings dedicated to mythological scenes (Danae, Adonis, Narcissus and Ganymede). The nudes painted by Michelangelo on the ceiling of the Sistine Chapel holding medallions and architectural elements here are seen three dimensionally and seem to hold up the cornices where the stories take place. It seems that inspiration for this place came from Francis I's gallery at Fontainebleau. From here you enter the actual apartment where each room contains a different frieze, painted as frescoes by artists who didn't go on to fame and fortune despite having shown good technique. From the life of Achilles we pass on to the celebration of Romulus, and finally to the story of Callisto and Proteus. But the tour keeps the most interesting surprise till last. In exactly the same place as the sessions of the Council of State take place, to the sides of the wooden benches where the thorniest of cases are often discussed, the walls offer a game of painted perspective, *trompe-l'oeil* bas-reliefs and false balustrades. People in costumes are peeking out from between the columns, spying on the goings on in the room. If at the time this was to amuse the Cardinal's guests, today this decoration seems almost to warn judges and lawyers who meet in this room. They have to remember that their work is closely scrutinized by all and, although taken within four walls, their decisions have an immediate effect on the outside. Along one of the walls a statue of Pompey is exhibited. Legend has it that it was beneath this very statue that Caesar was stabbed. Once more a tale of betrayal and political skullduggery, which is what they fight against in this room every day.

12 Palazzo Patrizi
where Portia and Francesco used to give memorable parties

For the visit
Piazza San Luigi de'Francesi, 37
You can visit the main floor of the building any day of the week, but you need to book calling n. 06 6869737 or writing an e-mail to patrizimontoro@gmail.com.
Own guide.
Entrance fee.

Amongst the paintings on show on the main floor at Palazzo Patrizi there is one that is truly curious, in which the Marquis Francesco Naro is shown sitting on a seat of velvet whilst holding in one hand a greyhound on a leash and in the other a white carnival mask with a severe expression. It is the mask of Cassandrino, a costume that the Marquis used to wear on the occasions of the parties that he and his wife Portia Patrizi held, and which were famous throughout Rome in the 18th century. Cassandrino is a representation of our modern satire, which pulled no punches regarding politicians and, at that time, Cardinals and nobility: whoever wore his mask was at liberty to say whatever they wanted, causing laughter amongst their audience. It is easy to imagine just how much fun Marquis Patrizi's performances were, to which the nobility of the city flocked. The guests met in the rooms which today still form the apartment on the main floor opposite San Luigi de' Francesi. Warm and welcoming rooms which preserve the feeling of a private house, custodian to antique paintings and some masterpieces, such as Guercino's *St. Jerome*, busy closing a letter with sealing wax. The intellectual Saint is hunched over his writing desk and reveals, in the shape of his body, a clear homage to Michelangelo (an identical painting is held in Palazzo Barberini).

It is only one of the celebrated paintings which make up this collection put together in the 17th century by Mariano Patrizi, a passionate friend to artists and a painter himself. Amongst the works he was able to procure, there was also Caravaggio's *Supper at Emmaus*, now held at the Pinacoteca di Brera, in Milan.

It often happens that in moments of financial difficulty a family has to sell it jewels, but fortunately for the Patrizi, they have not found themselves often in this situation. Insomuch as that today one of the rooms is still dominated by the *Statue of the Amazon*, a rare example of Roman sculpture copied from the Hellenistic original. The Hellenistic style is that particular taste developed under Alexander the Great, when Greek culture was mixed with all the populations the Macedonian leader held under his sway. Those impassive figures, perfect and without sentiment, born in Athens three centuries before, acquired a movement never seen before, capable of expressing and eliciting emotion. This is what we find in the *Patrizi Amazon*, who falls from a horse and finds herself contorted in a very unusual position. It doesn't represent the woman's vigour but rather, her fragility. Its presence here in the Patrizi collection shows how they were not your ordinary common or garden collectors, and knew well how to choose works from the most sought-after artists, even if they weren't necessarily all that famous. As in the case of the Muses painted on the ceiling of the Great Room, one of the rare Roman works by Francesco Solimena, an extraordinary Neapolitan Baroque painter. There was a secret passage that allowed the servants to pass from one room to another so as not to disturb the guests, to whom on social occasions the view of the private chapel was also hidden. Rather than a true chapel, it is an altar, hidden behind a wooden door that is still opened today for family ceremonial occasions such as baptisms or Easter and Christmas masses. In Rome it is one of the few private altars that still officiates masses, a privilege that could be due to the memory of the mythical founder of the family. It is said the Patrizis actually are the descendants of the patrician Giovanni to whom in a dream the Madonna spoke telling him to build a church on a spot where snow had fallen. This was the birth of the Basilica Santa Maria Maggiore, where still today the Patrizi Chapel keeps watch over the family tomb.

13 Palazzo Salviati
where poets used to meet in a secret garden

For the visit
Piazza della Rovere, 83
Usually the Palace can be visited on an early Friday afternoons, when the rooms have been left by the civil servants who regularly work there. The number to call to request a visit is 06 46913171, but at the CASD they will ask you to send a fax to n. 06 68307825, for the attention of the President of the Centro Alti Studi della Difesa, with the name and surname of the participating visitors and a proposed date. The personnel offer a guide service.
Free entrance.

Today Rome's Botanical Gardens are one of the most tranquil and elegant corners of the city, frequented for the most part by mothers with babies and few foreign tourists, who visit it after having seen the frescoes at Villa Farnesina and the paintings at Palazzo Corsini. And yet few people know that the Capital's first scientific garden was to be found at the opposite end of via Lungara, inside Palazzo Salviati. It was Pope Leo XIII in 1823 who listened to the numerous protests from the scholars of the University of Sant'Ivo at the Sapienza, who were complaining about not having a suitable place for their plant studies. At that time the Botanical Gardens of the University were, for almost two centuries, to be found behind the Fontanone dell'Acqua Paola, too far from the laboratories near Piazza Navona. In the 19th century it was thus decided to use as a treasure chest of trees and exotic plants the grounds belonging to the Palace, which had just been inherited by Marcantonio Colonna from his mother Zeffirina Salviati. It is at this point that a rare pepper tree was introduced to the garden, and is still today an attraction here that, despite its close proximity to the busiest part of the Lungotevere in Rome, still offers surprising tranquility. It could be for this particular aspect that Antonio Maria Salviati in 1699 transformed it to host meetings of the members of the Academy of Arcadia.

This group of intellectuals and poets were famous for having tried, between the 17th and 18th centuries, to stage a return to the origins of Greek and Latin culture through the penning and public readings of clear texts, simple in structure and their prevalent pastoral themes. The name of their association derives from the area of Greece considered to be an idealistic natural paradise. For them the Cardinal created a theatre of green where they could exchange ideas and recite their works. Their presence on via Lungara lasted only a few years as, already in 1707, the Arcadians had to move. Their performances today however are remembered in the form of the garden, where the seats and the stage are still visible. The highest point of the "little theatre" is home to a small monument to the fallen: it is in memory of the pupils of the Military School who fought in World War I, and is subtle sign revealing the current identity of Palazzo Salviati. The residence has been linked to military activity since 1849, when the French troops settled in the building in order to defend the Pope from the Republicans. It was actually only in 1883 that the Military College of Rome opened here, ancestor of the current Centro Alti Studi della Difesa (Centre for Higher Military Studies), which today still has its headquarters here.

Little or nothing remains of the period when the Palace was the private residence of Filippo Ardinari, the secret treasurer to Pope Leo X Medici. He had it planned by Giulio Romano, but the artist, a pupil of Raphael's, never actually touched the project, which was then extended and finished by Nanni di Baggio Bigio, upon Cardinal Salviati's request. He was the one who had the Chapel decorated, which still houses the frescoes created by Santi di Tito, a Florentine painter faithful to the rules of Mannerism. His scenes drawn from the Acts of the Apostles provide a beautiful contrast to the much more demanding frescoes, that Hannibal Brugnoli created in the 1880s century on the ceilings of the rooms on the ground floor, today used as a library. The Unified State had just been born, Rome was about to become for all intents and purposes the Capital of Italy and Palazzo Salviati is one of the most prestigious military buildings in the City. It was impossible not to dedicate some frescoes to the Risorgimento (the Unification of Italy). And so, on the ceilings we can see a procession of the Battles of S. Martino, Montebello, Pastrengo and Custoza, accompanied by representations of various corps from the Army: from Cavalry to the Bersaglieri (Infantry famous for their plumed hats). In the centre of the lowered vaults some papyrus plants are spreading, an elegant decorative element anticipating the Liberty style, already on the horizon. Nothing remains of the works of art that made up the famous Salviati collection: they have been merged with the Colonna and Borghese collections due to arranged weddings in an attempt to thwart the dispersion of the family wealth.

14 Casino del Bel Respiro

where you can reach the Vatican through a tunnel

For the visit
Via Aurelia Antica, 111
Today the Casino is part of the property of the Presidency of the Council of Ministers. Visits are possible only on a Saturday morning between 9 and 12. You need to send a fax to 06 67793905 or write an e-mail to: visite@governo.it. For further information call 06 67794555.
Own guide.
Free entrance.

The name of the small Villa desired by Camillo Pamphilj is not coincidental. The "bel respiro" (fresh air) to which it is dedicated calls immediately to mind the Roman westerly breeze, that light wind that, especially in the afternoon, comes from the west and cools the summer heat. Be it for its location on the western side of Rome, or because it was built on a small hill, the Casino today remains one of the most pleasant places in the Capital, where you seem to be in the middle of the countryside. This is perhaps the reason why Ghadafi, for his stay in Rome in 2009, chose to plant his tent right in the middle of its secret garden. We are in the heart of Villa Pamphilj, where Prince Camillo, abandoning his ecclesiastical career, decided to create a showcase to exhibit his own collection which he had enriched with antique statues after his marriage to Olimpia Aldobrandini. He consulted Francesco Borromini, who had worked for the family at Sant'Agnese in Agone, but the architect came up with a far too elaborate project. And not even the more classical Girolamo and Carlo Rainaldi could satisfy the Prince's needs. To obtain the final, definitive project, he had to turn to a sculptor: Alessandro Algardi, an artist from Emilia, who planned the edifice with the help of the landscape artist Giovan Francesco Grimaldi.

Algardi, creator of the superb bust of *Olimpia Pamphilj* and a portrait in marble of *Pope Innocent X*, came up with a design based on the Villa d'Este, a famous Renaissance residence which had become a benchmark for villas with gardens. For the Casino's decorations the closest models are instead Villa Medici and Villa Borghese, which contain a vast number of sculptures and bas-reliefs on the external façade. To display their culture and prestige, the Princes of that time never spared any ostentation for Greco-Roman pieces, represented both by original exhibits and copies of ancient sculptures. Proof of this obsessive interest in antiquity is the fact that the statues still present inside the Casino are mostly authentic works that Grimaldi had restored for the Pamphiljs. They come from properties that the Princes had around Rome or from discoveries inside the park.

The building's Central Salon, a circular room around which all the other rooms are to be found, is characterized by four niches holding as many statues of divinities, fruits of the salvaging and inventive work of Algardi. An Amazon was transformed into the Goddess Diana thanks to the addition of a dog, while Venus does not appear completely nude anymore, as she has been dressed in a drape in the 17th century. Above each character there is a bas-relief which recounts a mythological event (the death of Meleager, the hunt for the centaur Celidonio…), copies of sarcophagi placed on the external façade. It is so important for the owners to reconnect their family with the splendour of Ancient Rome, that they ask the artist to plan on the lower floor a room dedicated to "Roman customs". Thus we find sculptures in the round of *Apollo and Minerva*, reproductions of temples and of the Pantheon. Recent restorations have given back to these stuccoes their original colour, which was not white but pale pink and blue; a true rarity. As are certain examples of plant life found in the secret garden, which had lost its original design in order to be transformed into an Italian paddock. In one corner still lives a so-called "bald cypress", a plant from North America that loses its leaves in autumn. It represents, to an extent, the historical memory of recent events in the Casino, which in the 20th century was redone with frescoes and some moving of the walls, such as the one knocked down to create the dining room which today holds a very long table, useful for the official breakfasts held by the Presidency of the Council of Ministers, to whom the building has been entrusted. Small secrets that only the custodians know about, the only ones to have seen the over 1.5 kilometer long tunnel that connects the Casino to the Vatican, an escape route created for the Popes when the building was still outside of the city. (I would like to thank here Dr. Ivana Corsetti)

15 Palazzo Rondinini
where a Marquis kept Michelangelo's famous Pietà

For the visit
Via del Corso, 518
The Circolo degli Scacchi opens for visits requested by groups from cultural associations only on the last Saturday of the month.
To make a request call 06 3210543 or 06 3213804 or send a fax to 06 3610209.
Own guide.
Free entrance.

On his *Travels through Italy* Goethe dedicated many pages to Rome, where he stayed for more than a year and a half on via del Corso (where today you can find the museum called the Casa di Goethe), directly opposite Palazzo Rondinini (also called Rondanini), a building which only a few years before, the Marquis Giuseppe Rondinini had bought to show his collection of antique finds and works of art. The German writer tells of his frequent visits to the Palace, where, most of all, he was fascinated by a mask of the Medusa hanging in the courtyard. It seems indeed that the entire architecture of the building was conceived in order to exalt the beauty of sculptures, the stuccoes and the paintings which went to make up one of the most celebrated collections of the era. The jewel in the crown of this collection was the *Pietà*, sculpted by Michelangelo at the end of his career in such a stylized form as to earn the disdain of the Palace's owners in the 19th century. Consequently, at the first opportunity, Count Sanseverino, on having just come into possession of the Palace, sold the sculpture to the city of Milan (today it is one of the attractions at Castello Sforzesco). In fact, today the residence's main decorative works date back to the 18th century, when Marquis Rondinini bought the palace where Giuseppe Cesari (called the Cavalier d'Arpino) had lived.

The famous painter, alongside who even Caravaggio had worked, had managed to put together a prestigious dwelling, even cited in 17th century guides to Rome.

Intending to create a Palace worthy of his collection, Rondinini extended the building and erased any trace of the painter's house. He had a courtyard built rich with bas-reliefs and sculptures, in line with the 18th century taste for antiquities, he had a grand stairway built and a series of rooms on the main floor, still perfectly preserved today. After numerous changes of hands, at the beginning of the 20th century the Palace became the property of the Banca di Agricoltura, now a part of the Montepaschi Group. And it is the bank who in 1990 welcomes the Nuovo Circolo degli Scacchi, which today is custodian and manager of the most important floor. Between fresco landscapes with *Scenes of Tobias*, allegories enriched by *rocaille* cornicing and tasteful carpeting, the apartment is one of the most coherent rococo environments in Rome. With inlaid furniture, precious marbles on the walls and marble flooring with geometric designs, every corner breathes elegance and luxury, apart from the rooms that have been conceived as museum-rooms to exhibit works of art. Here a more severe and essential taste pervades, leaving space for the sculptures, for instance the *Fountain of Venus* which rains down upon an artificial rock within a niche, or the pictures of picturesque ruins surrounded by elegant white stucco. Many others, however, have been lost: 18th-century guides tell of paintings by Titian, Raphael, Correggio and Domenichino, today dispersed throughout the world, like the *Medusa* admired by Goethe, now one of the principal pieces in Munich's Glyptothek.

16 Palazzo Antici Mattei di Giove
where the architect copied an ancient Roman house

For the visit
Via Michelangelo Caetani, 32
Visits can be arranged through the Centre for American Studies, calling 06 68801613 or sending a fax to 06 68307256 or an e-mail to info@centrostudiamericani.org.
Own guide.
Entrance fee.

This is one of the Palaces making up the famous "Insula Mattei", an entire block made up of five houses belonging to as many members of the same family. It is one of the largest residences in Rome, and capable of competing with the Pope's dwellings in the Vatican and on the Quirinal. It represents a kind of "imperial palace" which held extraordinary treasures and was built on the foundations of the *cavea* of Lucio Cornelio Balbo's ancient theatre (1st Century B.C.). This setting was not in any way coincidental. Between via Papalis, which the Pope used to take in order to get to Campidoglio, and via Mercatoria, between the Tiber and the important trade areas of Banchi Vecchi and Campo de' Fiori, this architectural complex occupied a strategic position. During the 16th century, the Mattei family put into action a precise real estate strategy, thanks to which they were able to acquire a series of buildings which allowed them to create a compact centre for their activities, organized into workshops, warehouses, laboratories and residences. In a census carried out in the 1520s they were shown to be amongst the Pope's biggest contributors, second only to the powerful Cesarini. Over time their needs for a status symbol prevailed over those of functionality and the Mattei family began to transform their properties into patrician palaces, inviting the most famous artists of the era to come and work there.

The last to see the light was Palazzo Mattei di Giove, built by Asdrubale Mattei, who entrusted the project to Maderno. He was the maestro, one of the most important architects of the Baroque, who devised a majestic courtyard on three levels, decorated completely with bas-reliefs and ancient statues, the only ones that remain from the family's extraordinary collection, today dispersed around the world. Crossing the open space where a fountain pouring water into a sarcophagus decorated with two leonine heads is still active, a grand staircase leads to the first floor. Today, the main floor of the Palace is divided up between various institutes and the most interesting rooms host the Italian Centre for American Studies. Some of the most illustrious artists of the 17th century worked in these rooms, recounting the stories of the fathers from the Old Testament. In his choice between pagan and religious subjects, Asdrubale preferred the latter. Already at the entrance, we find Moses thanking the Lord for the safe passage across the Red Sea, while in the adjacent rooms Francesco Albani painted *Jacob Asleep* and Domenichino portrayed *Jacob and Rachel at the fountain* between *trompe l'oeil* stucco work. The most important work is, however, the Gallery, where Pietro da Cortona created the *Tales of Solomon*, while Giovanni Lanfranco is attributed with the *Stories of Joseph* and *Elijah in a chariot*.

At the beginning of the 19th century, the male line of the Mattei di Giove family died out. The last heir, Marianna, married Carlo Teodoro Antici di Recanati, who acquired his wife's surname. As luck would have it, Antici was also the mother of Leopardi who, for some months between 1822 and 1823, stayed at the Palazzo Mattei di Giove. His presence seems to have brought good luck for the building's future, as today it has become a prestigious cultural magnet.

17 Palazzo Chigi
where a fountain merges mountains, stars and oak leaves

For the visit
Piazza Colonna, 370
Visits to Palazzo Chigi take place on Saturday mornings.
The employees of the Presidency of the Council of Ministers act as guides on a route that takes about an hour and a half. Unfortunately some of the truly beautiful rooms cannot be seen, but the visit is still worthwhile.
To book, call
06 67793471
or send a fax to
06 67794122
or an e-mail to
visite@governo.it.
Free entrance.

Few Roman buildings such as Palazzo Chigi still show today evidence of the traces of its different phases of construction. For example, looking up high at the cornicing, it is possible to see a difference between the part that were done when the Aldobrandini were the owners, decorated with a star and a rake, and that done under the Chigi family, characterized by stars and mountains. In fact, the question of family in this residence is even more complicated, as the Chigis (who came to Rome from Siena in the 16th century and reached the height of their power a century later with Pope Alexander VII) under Giulio II in 1506 became mixed with the Della Rovere family and in the 19th century also inherited the Albani name.

This is demonstrated well by the fountain found in line with the entrance gate on via del Corso (at one time the main entrance): around the large mask branches of oak (Della Rovere) are circling, while above we can see eight mountains (Albani) and the star (Chigi). The Palace, which today is the main seat of the Presidency of the Council of Ministers, arose from the initiative of Pietro Aldobrandini who, in 1578, acquired a house on via del Corso and decided to begin expansionary works towards Piazza Colonna. The works went on for two generations until, in 1659, during the pontificate of Alexander VII, Olimpia Aldobrandini sold it to the Chigi family.

It was only in the 18th century that the door finally opened onto the Piazza and the decoration on the second floor was done, where we have the famous Salone d'Oro (Gold Room), created to celebrate nuptials of Sigismondo Chigi and Maria Flaminia Odescalchi. Following along the Scalone d'Onore (staircase of Honour), once adorned with many statues which today have been dispersed, we enter into the Sala delle Galere (Galley Room), which takes its name from the nautically themed stucco panel above the door, testimony to the period in which the building was the seat of the Ministry of Colonies. This Room precedes the antechamber of the room where the Council of Ministers meets. To the sides of the door we can see two world maps, one terrestrial the other celestial, while the fresco frieze on the ceiling shows an allegorical theme and the coats of arms of the Chigi and the Sayn, who were united by marriage in the 19th century. You could think that the Sala del Consiglio (Council Room) would be the most prestigious in the Palace, but actually this is not so, as the ministers sit around a circular table that comes with a number of seats and which changes with every government, inside a room with an undecorated wooden ceiling. There are some mythological figures on the Baroque frieze, whilst on the walls two tapestries from the school of Rubens are hung. Nothing at all to do with the *grisailles* in the Vice President's antechamber or the maritime paintings by Manglard in what is today the President's Breakfast Room. Here a fake portico opens up to the view to a natural landscape with ships ploughing through the sea and rocks that frame the corners - an invention that connects well with the Neoclassical style Pompeian decoration on the walls. The rooms are in a perfect state of preservation thanks to the restorations that took place in the '90s. In particular, on the top floor, the amazing condition of the wooden shelving in the Library is surprising: these are the originals from the Chigi Library built in the 17th century to hold the volumes collected by Cardinal Flavio Chigi. While today the books have been absorbed into the Vatican Library, the rooms still hold the original structures from the period. A true rarity.

18 Villa Madama
where a fountain reminds us of Hanno, the elephant

For the visit

Via di Villa Madama
The Villa today is entrusted to the Ministry of Foreign Affairs and is used on State occasions by the Government.
You can book visits 15 days in advance, but confirmation depends on government commitments.
Call 06 36914284
or send a fax to
06 36913401
or an e-mail to:
cerimoniale.segreteria@esteri.it.
You will have to send the list of all participants with personal details and the number of an ID document.
Own guide.
Free entrance.

Rome could have been very different if some of the planned architectural projects had actually gone ahead. Who knows what via Giulia would be today if Pope Julius II had carried out the "administrative hub" which he had in mind (but the Tiber proved to be too much of a threat to the stability of the buildings). Who knows what Piazza Navona would look like if Bernini hadn't pilfered the job from Borromini. The same thoughts occur when we look at Monte Mario, the hill which may have got its name from "mare", the sea, as already in ancient times, fossilized shells had been found there in the ground. Up until the end of the 19th century, one could breath the air of open countryside here. For centuries it was a popular spot for walks in the woods and a favourite location for the construction of extraordinary villas, such as Villa Madama.

It is a shame that Cardinal Giulio de'Medici's plans for the Villa encountered so many problems and was never actually finished. With the election of his cousin to the papacy (Leo X), the Cardinal became engrossed in a magnificent initiative which would have included the entire slope of the hill down to the Tiber. He gave the project to Raphael, at that time head of the St. Peter's Foundry, but unfortunately the artist died prematurely in 1520 causing a first unexpected halt. Even when the Cardinal became Pope Clement VII, in 1523, things did not get better, as in 1527 Rome underwent its famous "sacking" at the hands of Charles V's Landsknechts and Villa Madama, as was true for many other projects in the city, remained a plan barely touched upon.

Only the chronicles and some designs from the time allow us to imagine the monumental construction which should have occupied the hill with terraces descending right down to the river. From this Renaissance project there remains today a fabulous lodge remains, which opens onto a secret garden decorated with frescoes by Giulio Romano and stucco works by

Giovanni di Udine. The rest, the upper levels and, above all, the façade are the result of works commissioned to Marcello Piacentini by the Dentice family of Frasso, who came into possession of the Villa in 1925. It couldn't have been easy for a modern architect to lay hands on a work by Raphael, even though he was trained in the great architectural works of the past. He decides to leave the brick structuring on the façade visible which Raphael would have wanted to cover in precious marble and limits himself to creating a spiral staircase leading to the first floor, in order to render this extraordinary building more habitable. In fact, leaving aside the top floor, where Piacentini laid out the more intimate rooms, the rest of the Villa is an extraordinary monument inspired by the famous imperial villas from antiquity, above all Villa Adriana. As soon as you enter it hits you that the dominating colour is white, because of the stuccoes that cover the walls and the ceiling.

While moving towards the garden, three huge vaults host multi-coloured frescoes painted by students of Raphael. The themes of the decorations, to the elaboration of which the humanist Paolo Giovio contributed, draw from myths linked with nature and the four fundamental elements, as recounted by Ovid in his *Metamorphoses*: water is represented by *Neptune's chariot*, earth by *Pluto and Proserpina*, air by *Juno*, while Jupiter is loving Ganymede in order to represent fire. All around them, we have the signs of the zodiac and the famous grotesques, transformed by the very same artists into fashionable decorations for the interior, inspired by the discoveries under the Oppian Hill. The entire cycle of frescoes, one of the richest and most complex in Rome, aimed at celebrating the heights of prosperity reached by the city thanks to the governing of the Medici popes, under the protection of the stars and nature which, upon close inspection, is represented by the ancient divinities. This strange role exchange between pagan divinities and the Christian God can also be seen at Villa Madama, which never appears in this residence of cardinals. This shouldn't surprise as it occurred regularly that, above all in country residences, it was preferable to surround yourself with imagery linked to literature and leisure, as classical culture was considered to be. And this is why the Pope allowed a fountain to be dedicated in his garden to his favourite "pet": an elephant. Made of shells and shellfish fossils, the fountain was to commemorate Hanno, the pachyderm from Ceylon given as a present to Pope Leo X by the Portuguese Ambassador. On his brief stay in Rome (he died after only three years from his arrival due to the city's overly dry climate), the elephant conquered the entire population of the city and was inspiration for poems and works of art. What struck most was his intelligence shown through the games he played with water and acrobatics when he was paraded through the streets of Rome.

On the day of his arrival, upon descending from the ship that had brought him from India, the animal stopped in front of the Pope, rubbing his slippers with his trunk, then, well trained, took up water from a silver container and sprayed the crowd that had rushed to see him.

They understood immediately that he had already been taught to give blessings.

19 Palazzo Baldassini
where Garibaldi announced the new embankments for the Tiber

For the visit
Via delle Coppelle, 35
The Istituto Luigi Sturzo offers the chance to visit the Palace, preferably in groups and accompanied by a guide.
To agree a time for the visit, call
06 6840421 or send a fax to 06 68404244 or an e-mail to:
info.segretariogenerale @sturzo.it.
Own guide.
Free entrance.

Palazzo Baldassini is one of the clearest examples of the return to fashion of classical architecture in 16th century Rome. The rediscovery of the Vitruvian texts, which had revealed to the Romans the secrets of the Greek temples and dictated the criteria for the construction of the *domus* of the rich patricians, translated easily into antique-style palaces and churches. Among the first artists to interpret this Roman *nouvelle vague* was Antonio da Sangallo, the star of some of the city's most important works at the beginning of the 16th century.

At Palazzo Baldassini the architect was inspired by the structure of the *domus*: the atrium, around which circled the entire patrician dwelling, became the inner courtyard, which was the main source of light for the rooms.

In fact, all around small streets and alleys open

up and the buildings are leaning on each other, as in medieval times. The idea to upset the orientation of the rooms and create the main fronts facing onto the courtyard was truly a stroke of genius. The courtyard also became the building's main representation area, where meaningful decorative elements would be placed. At Palazzo Baldassini, a frieze runs the height of the stringcourse: in the metopes (the same ones from the Greek temples) liturgical subjects alternate with the family crest and a small elephant, a homage to Hanno, the elephant received as a gift by Pope Leo X in the same period (see Villa Madama). To achieve greater luminosity even on the main floor and, above all, to provide an open-air space to those who didn't want to go down to street level, one side of the courtyard was turned into a large loggia. Fundamentally, ancient architecture enjoyed its great success because the solutions invented by the ancient Romans still corresponded very well to the needs for functionality and comfort of the new nobility, who were expanding their business affairs in the shadow of the papal court. The Neapolitan legal practitioner Melchiorre Baldassini was no different, he invited the new generation of artists, forged in Raphael's work sites, to come and work at his new house. Names that go on to become famous for being creators of extraordinary cycles of frescoes and remarkable inventions, such as the "stoves", small bathrooms that at the beginning of the 16th century started popping up in the noblemen's palaces. Palazzo Baldassini also has one, decorated by Perin del Vaga with mythological scenes and subjects inspired, obviously, by water. While the most famous "stove", the one belonging to Cardinal Bibbiena in the Vatican Palaces, was dedicated to Venus, this one on via delle Coppelle shows Narcissus looking at his reflection in the water, together with a frieze showing crabs and other marine creatures. It is perhaps the most elegant corner of a series of rooms where Giovanni da Udine, Polidoro da Caravaggio and Perin del Vaga seem to have given the best of themselves. Exotic and fantastic animals accompany the figures of divinities, metaphors for the four elements, and a swarm of birds, owls, mice, hedgehogs and squirrels. A room that was considered more than appropriate by Don Luigi Sturzo's friends, who bought and restored it in order to transform it into the seat of the Library and of the philosopher's manuscripts.
Among the illustrious inhabitants of the Palace we must mention Garibaldi. It seems that the General resided here, when, after the unification of Italy, he became prime mover of the construction of the Tiber's embankments in order to render Rome a safer and healthier place, undisturbed by the demolitions that the work would cause.

20 Villa Lante
where a cruel soldier left his mark on the wall

For the visit
Passeggiata del Gianicolo, 10
Access to the Villa is possible weekdays during office hours. The Institutum often opens it for cultural events (concerts, conferences).
To arrange a visit call 06 68801674 or send a fax to 06 68802349. Own guide. Free entrance.

«A dì 6 de magio 1527 fo la presa di Roma» (On 6th May 1527 Rome was taken). Who knows with what satisfaction the landsknecht (mercenary soldier) marked his passing through by scratching on the wall of the salon in Villa Lante. The "sacking" of Rome was one of the most nefarious episodes for the city, but at the same time one of the most exhilarating for those who, like the mercenary soldiers, were looking for fame and an adrenalin rush. That piece of graffiti has suitably been left visible on the frescoed wall of this jewel of Roman Mannerism, a small villa which, within a few square metres, brings into question all the rules of Renaissance architecture. The experts have now agreed that the author of this project was Giulio Romano, Raphael's favourite pupil (with whom he has to contend regarding the attribution of many works…). He was the one to design a perfect cube, in which, however, the rules of symmetry were not respected. Not only are the proportions between the two floors irregular, but inside, the main room is moved to one side, contravening all the Vitruvian traditions. Not yet content, the architect then extended one of the building's walls with a loggia facing the city, to best take advantage of the panoramic position on the Gianicolo hill.

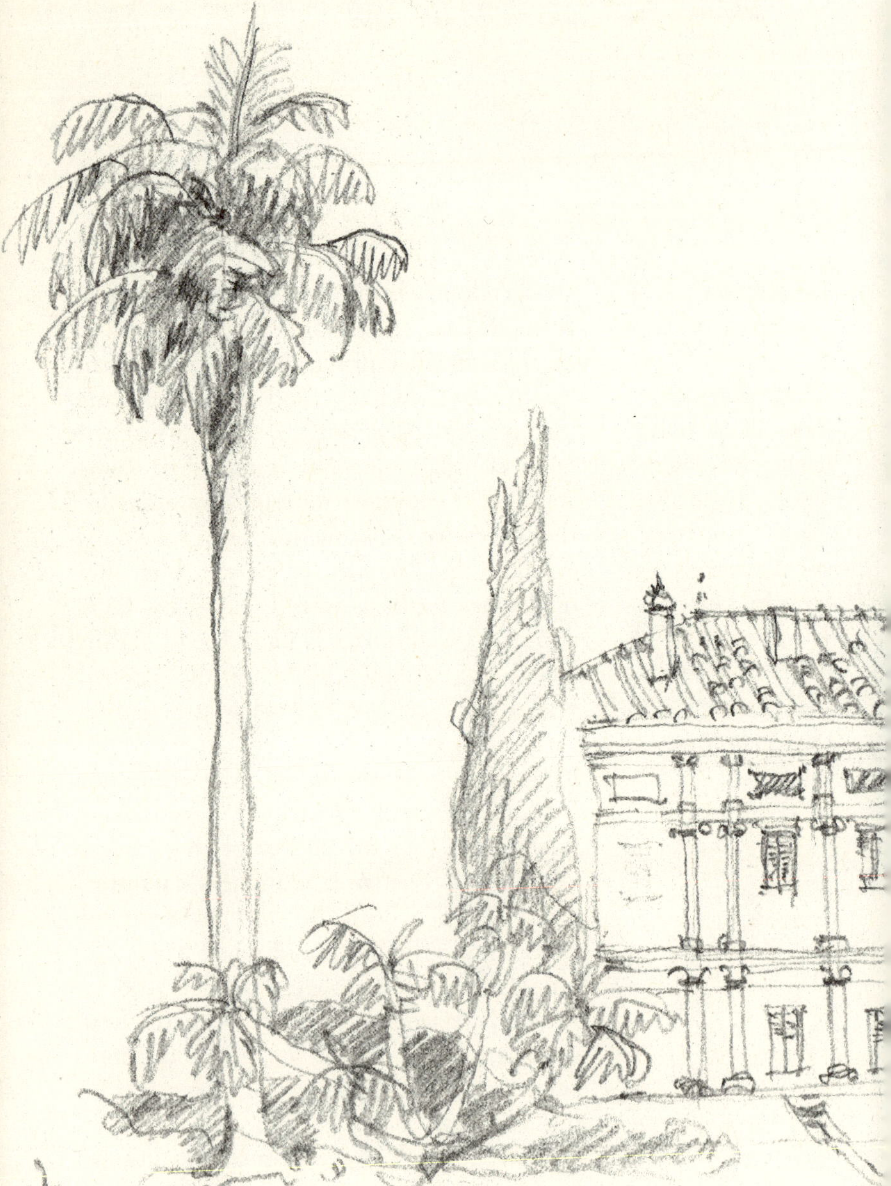

Even today, looking out from Villa Lante is a breathtaking experience which adds to the strange atmosphere generated by an environment realized using ancient calculations (it seems that the unit of measurement for the loggia is the root of 2!).

The choice to lengthen the typical Palladian arch, in such as way as to create a classical opening, but at the same time lively with an alternating game (arch – beam – arch – beam – arch) was also unusual. This large terrace, which at one time was open towards the slope, contains a completely white stucco decoration: the suspicion remains that in the 19th century the original colours were obliterated. The themes which inspired the figures do not correspond to a coherent narrative cycle. There are chariots, figures and, at the top, the Moon, the Sun and Jupiter: the stars *par excellence* who watch and celebrate the lavishness of the Medici and Baldassarre Turini. He is the legal practitioner, close to the gentlemen of Florence, who commissioned the construction of the Villino, which was never destined to be lived in, but to be more of a meeting place for intellectuals, artists and friends, in one of the most salubrious spots in Rome.

At the time he decided to realize this project, Turini was Pope Leo X's "calendar man", one of the most important figures in Rome, his job being to "stamp the date" on the Pope's provisions in order to render them definitively enforceable. It is a shame that, as often happens, the inheritors of great fortunes don't have the same passion for works of art obtained through no effort. This was the case at Villa Lante too: Turini's nephew is not at all interested in enjoying the outdoors on the Gianicolo and decides to rent the villa out and later, in 1551, to sell it to the Lante family. On buying the building, the Lante family did not make any great changes as the decoration was practically finished.

In the salon, the frescoes show the history of the Gianicolo Hill with scenes and mythological characters such as Janus and Saturn, who meet on the Janiculum. It seems that the main part of the decoration was removed in the 19th century when the villa passed to the Sacro Cuore (Sacred Heart) religious order: the nuns considered it unsuitable for the children in their crèche. These frescoes today can be found at Palazzo Zuccari. The Borghese coat of arms however has remained in place, it can be found on the vault and is related to the visit in 1608 by Pope Paul V, who was related to the Lante family. These merchants from Pisa are the protagonists in an unstoppable three-century-long ascension on the social and political scene: in 1640, when Pope Urban VIII occupied a part of their land on the hill to erect Rome's defensive wall, they received as compensation the villa at Bagnaia. A measure taken due to their influential position in Roman circles, which was brought down a peg or two at the beginning of the 19th century when financial difficulties obliged the Lante family to cede the property to Camillo Borghese. From this point on began a series of ownership changes which in 1950 culminated in the acquisition of the property by the Institutum Romanun Finlandiae, one of the many foreign institutions that offer to their artists and scholars a foothold in the Eternal City. It is thanks to them and to the Finnish Embassy at the Holy See that Villa Lante remains today an almost intact jewel.

21 Villa Barberini
where the nymph plaited her hair

For the visit
Borgo S.Spirito, 20
To arrange a visit you need to send an e-mail to canisioroma@gmail.com or telephone 06 689771 and ask to speak with the Istituto San Pietro Canisio.

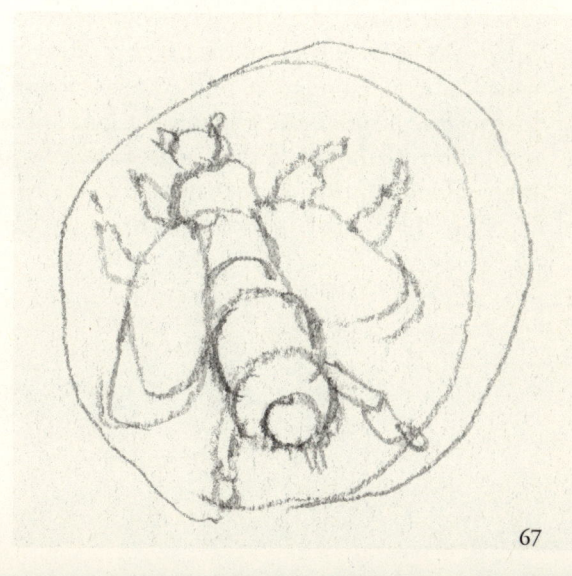

If one didn't know that on the other side of those high walls there was a villa designed, amongst others, by Bernini, they would think that the trees above the walls of Borgo Santo Spirito were merely the last traces of the Gianicolo Woods. As a matter of fact, the height of the wall was justified by a news item and not the need to hold up the hill: it was built to prevent the mental patients institutionalized in the Villa from climbing up and perhaps falling and doing permanent damage to themselves. At the end of the 19th century, before becoming a Jesuit residence, Villa Barberini was in fact given to the mental institution on via della Lungara and, given the amenities of the place and the quality of the building, was used for the care of the most wealthy patients. A strange fate for a cardinal's residence which had, since Taddeo Barberini acquired it in 1641, experienced many ups and downs in its history. At the time, the land held a small building, known in Rome as the Casino della Palma, starting point for a factory which had to deal with the problem of a very steep slope. The architects to whom the project was assigned, Domenico Castelli and Goivanni Antonio Bonazzini, decided to level the ground and create a building that would take advantage of the natural height difference. As often happens, change at the top created tremors in the political and social structure of the State and, with the election of Innocent X Pampilj in 1645 to the papacy, Taddeo Barberini had to find shelter in France, were he died two years later. As a consequence, works on the Villa were interrupted.

Eight years later it would be his son, Carlo, to recommence them. It was at this time that Bernini created a fountain for the Villa in which a nymph twists her hair whilst in the act of drying it. This gesture causes water to come out in "very fine spurts". All we know of the fountain now is that it was sold in England in the 18th century, as were probably many of the other sculptures that decorated the park. Of the old splendour only some of the internal decorations remain, where putti hold up the heraldic symbol of the Barberini with the distinctive bees, whilst on the vault in the salon flower garlands, putti and exotic birds hover.

22 Villino Gamberini
where you fall into Istanbul

For the visit
Via Palestro, 28
To visit the Villa you need to write an e-mail to: roma.be@libero.it, preferably in English. Own guide. Free Entrance.

Whoever has studied the history of art knows that one of the most often seen dates in Roman palace decorations is 1571, the year when the Papal fleet at Lepanto managed to stem the Turkish invasion. The Muslim threat was sent packing and in the papal residences the "Turk in chains" became one of the most frequent themes. It would take centuries to restore Islam its former dignity as an ancient and unique culture of profound values and refined aesthetics. The 19th century, with its taste for the exotic and orientalist painters, constituted a turning point in the relationship between Christian and Islamic iconography. This could also be the reason why Countess Lodigiani Gamberini accepts to sell the Villa to the Ottoman Empire in 1887 for the sum of 950 thousand Lira (the equivalent real estate value of 5 million euros today). Or perhaps, more simply, at that time in Rome there were very few people who could afford such an expense for a building of just over two thousand covered square metres. Obviously, the value was not linked solely to the dimensions but also to the decoration of the rooms, which were commissioned by Count Giuseppe Gamberini at the beginning of 1880. It is one of the first post-unification private works to be done, where the owner wanted to be surrounded by gilded stuccoes in a pure Rococo style, in a complete contrast to the extremely sober and linear exterior of the building.

When the Turkish ambassador entered the Villa, he must have felt at home: the atmosphere was very reminiscent of the rooms in Beylerbeyi Palace in Istanbul, one of the most sumptuous on the Asiatic bank of the Bosporus. The building today still hosts the seat of the Turkish Ambassadorial delegation, one of the most important places for promoting a constructive dialogue with the cultures of our Eastern neighbours.

23 Villino Ximenes
where an artist made the largest sculpture of Rome

For the visit
Via Cornelio Celso, 1
The villa today is the home to the Istituzione Teresiana, which, in addition to the nuns, also houses some female students. Visits are allowed only by appointment, by calling 06 4402645.

Art Nouveau in France, *Jugendstil* in Germany, Secession in Austria, *Modern Style* in England, Modernism in Italy: at the beginning of the 20th century, the style more commonly known as Liberty underwent an unexpected development in Europe and touched all the creative disciplines, from painting to architecture, from illustration to design.

In Italy, where it was limited to the first decade of the century, it saw the forming of artists who had the chance to test their talents on highly representative official public works and also on some more intimate private works. This was the case of Ettore Ximenes, a sculptor originally from Sicily, who in Rome worked on and created the *Quadriga* (chariot drawn by 4 horses) surmounting the Palace of Justice, as well as the group of *Diritto* (Law) on the Vittoriano.

Enormous sculptures, which he worked on in his studio in Piazza Galeno, in the new Salario district, where he constructed a villa for himself, devising everything down to the smallest details. A comparison between the official sculptures created for the Roman monuments with the precious decorations in his house allows us to gauge his capacity to move from a bombastic, pompous and melodramatic style to a more refined and elegant one, using precious materials and more intimate themes. On the outside of Villa Ximenes a frieze runs where great artists form two processions towards the Altar of the Arts: an almost religious representation of the artist's work, which even at that time was already assuming a somewhat sacerdotal and ascetic tint.

Even though above the *ara artium* a Madonna has been placed now (the building is currently home to a religious institute), all the rest of the decorations are characterized by classical and naturalistic themes, such as the extraordinary palm trees that crown the façade overlooking the Piazza and the stunning white eagle, accompanied by putti holding up flourishing festoons. The natural element is known to be the most recurring in the so called "floral style" and this immediately becomes clear as soon as you enter inside. The Vestibule is an enchanted forest, which gives onto a Drawing Room where the stucco work imitates tree branches and leaves. In the highest part on one side of the room, Ximenes wanted to recount a brief period of the history of Italian art, portraying Bernini, Urban VIII, Cardinal Mazzarino and a bust of Louis XIV. A clear homage to the Baroque, the first style to transform stone into organic material through architecture and sculpture. Who knows why he didn't portray Borromini, who on this subject was far more daring...

The room on the other side of the entrance holds, still intact, Ximenes' Breakfast Room which the artist chose to decorate with *panelling* inlaid with vine branches and flowers. This is where the most elegant taste of Liberty shines through: no structural element exists that can't be turned into a decorative element. Each shelf, each door jamb and knocker is an excuse to bring a plant to life, all the better if it is rare and exotic.

In the Villino almost everything has remained intact, but unfortunately the space occupied by the artist's studio in the centre of the building has been reordered and is no longer visible. The entire central area, where there is an *auditorium* now on the basement level and further rooms on the floors above, once made up a large environment, several metre in height. It was accessed through an enormous door, which was connected outside to a ramp through which the artist's sculptures, destined for some of the most important monuments in Italy and the world, were carried out. A modern Vulcan's forge.

24 Palazzo della Marina
where we can meet the great navigators

For the visit
Piazzale della Marina
The General Staff organize guided visits of the Palace on the first and third Saturday of the month between 9 and 5 o'clock. Bookings can be made calling 06 36805251 or 06 36804863. Guide service available.
Free entrance.

When Rome became the capital of Italy, a new construction fever broke out all over the city, the biggest since the papal constructions of the 16th century transformed its medieval appearance. It started with occupying large tracts of land outside the old walls, first of all in the sector to the East (Salario and Nomentano), and then to the North and the West (Flaminio and Prati).

The reference models for building are those from the North of Italy, above all Turin, imbued with the resurgence of the neo-Renaissance layout. On rarer occasions the Liberty taste insinuated itself, however, it found itself up against Rome's more classical and stricter tradition. It was on this Classical vein that the project for the Palazzo della Marina came along, for which an extremely scenic position is chosen, on one side facing over the Tiber and on the other the foothills of Villa Borghese.

A short distance from Piazza del Popolo rises an enormous complex in which the Italian fleet is celebrated, which is ready shortly thereafter to demonstrate great skill in international conflicts. As often happens on official occasions for the armed forces, a certain rhetorical spirit dominates even in the decoration of the palace, which prompted the Italian Government to choose the most precious marbles and heroic imagery to motivate their sea faring army. It suffices to look at the title of the image that decorates the ceiling of the main room, the Sala dei Marmi (Marble Room): «*La nave di Roma nuovamente sospinta in mare dalle giovani energie della stirpe*» (The ship of Rome launched again to sea by the bloodlines' youthful energy).

The painting vaguely brings to mind Théodore Géricault's *The Raft of the Medusa*, with the addition of the imperial eagles on the rostrum. It was painted in 1928 (seventeen years after the decision to build the palace!) by Antonio Calcagnadoro and is perhaps the most important of the artist's works who, amongst his other merits, can boast that he was the teacher of Mario Mafai.

Around the room, decorated with ionic pilasters with gold-plated capitals, runs a frieze with fake bronze stucco work and maritime emblems. In the entrance hall lies perhaps the most curious finding. The Ministry holds a memento of the most important Italian navigators in history, represented by statues and paintings showing the faces of Christopher Columbus, Vettor Pisani, up to Marcantonio Colonna and the Venetians Sebastiano Venier and Lazzaro Mocenigo.

25 Casino di Villa Carpegna
where ancient and contemporary art meet

For the visit
Piazza di Villa Carpegna
The Quadrennial provides a guided visit service which takes place on Tuesdays and Fridays and need to be booked at least 24 hours in advance on 06 9774531 or via e-mail: relazioniesterne@quadriennaledirom a.org. Entrance fee.

It is thanks to the restorations in the eighties that the frescoes in the Gallery of the small noble house at Villa Carpegna came to light. Until that point, the building was considered a simple and elegant example of Baroque architecture, destined more for countryside entertainment than hosting official occasions. However, Cardinal Gaspare Carpegna was not put off by the small dimensions of the place and transformed the vineyard into a site to exhibit his treasures. Here, Pietro Francesco Garolli was commissioned to paint the estate belonging to the Carpegna family in Montefeltro, gracious landscapes appearing behind balustrades and columns, in a vaguely neo-Renaissance style. The artist plays an interesting game with the design of the columns, which create views at the same height as the doors and windows, which thus seem to be absorbed into the fresco. At close proximity they are reminiscent of the walls in Palazzo Farnesina on via Lungara. Above the doors reliefs and *trompe-l'oeil* heads can be found. With the passage of the Villino's ownership to the Falconieri, in the 19th century the building acquires another decorated room on the ground floor. It is a small salon painted in the "Pompeian" style, an atmosphere that had by then been fashionable for decades, following the discovery of the ruins of Pompei in the mid-18th century. The ceiling vault shows the heraldic symbols of the family, accompanied by putti carrying tools for hunting and fishing.

On one wall a girl appears, dancing on a terrace and behind her a panorama with a far off horizon opens up: an illusionary effect that was very fashionable at the time.

It is around this time that another farmhouse is erected next to the Casino, its main function being that of agricultural store. Everything changes when Villa Carpegna passes to the hands of the Dutch baroness, Caterina Von Scheyns: the noblewoman not only transforms the garden by adding colourful flowers, above all peonies, but also dedicates herself to the decoration of the two buildings. In the Casino she introduces a floor mosaic and Liberty decorations in tempera, whilst she turns the farmhouse into a salon for meetings with intellectuals and artists. This is the period when the plaster exterior takes on its characteristic red colour, harmonizing with white stuccoes and floral elements. From a country retreat the Villino becomes a true noble residence.

Since 2004 it has been the home of the Fondazione Quadriennale, which for a short while now has been organizing exhibitions of work by contemporary artists in the historic spaces it has at its disposal. An excellent initiative, which contrasts ancient art with contemporary one as only in Rome is it possible to do.

26 Palazzo Montecitorio
where every Saturday the lottery was drawn

For the visit
Piazza di Monte Citorio, 33 (Sundays)
Piazza del Parlamento (all other days)
Palazzo Montecitorio opens to the public the first Sunday of every month. It is however possible to request a visit on other days by calling 06 67604565 or 06 67603875.
For visits by adults you need to be in groups and member of a cultural organization (of which it is necessary to present the bylaws).
It is advisable to request visits outside the high and festive seasons, when school groups are not scheduled. Guide service available.
Free entrance.

Who knows if in the 18th century the public lottery reached the jackpot heights of the Superenalotto (the Italian lottery). It was definitely one of the most popular events in Rome, described in some exhilarating passages by Stendhal in his *Walks in Rome*. From the terrace on the main façade, the numbers were read out to the crowd gathered below in the piazza, which even at that time was slightly raised. The slight height difference of the ground could be the origin of its name, Montecitorio, as it seems that it was formed by the accumulation of earth and rubbish coming from the reclamation of the nearby Campo Marzio. The ancient name would have therefore been Mons Acceptorius, from which derived Montecitorio. We don't known about any major construction in this place before the 16th century, probably because of the close proximity to the Tiber, which would have made building difficult in this area. It is only in the 17th century that works started on an important palace. In that period, Nicolò Ludovisi was the owner of the structure. Hearing of the upcoming building site, Bernini set out to obtain the contract for its planning. Just as he had already done for Piazza Navona, he made a small model of his project in silver and gave it to the Prince's wife. She was the one who acquired the contract for him, which the artist fulfilled by creating an imposing convex façade to follow and highlight the morphology of the land. Bernini did not finish the project due to the death of the patron. The following occupant was Pope Innocent XII Pignatelli, who had a trusted architect, Carlo Fontana, and it was he who took Bernini's post and intervened, above all, on the organization of the building's interior and the courtyard, in order to transform the palace into the papal Curia, where the Pope's tribunals would be held for more than a century. The most garish addition is the bell tower which is surmounted by a gyrating bronze sculpture with two wings and an hour glass: Time. The building's fate as an administrative seat never deserts Palazzo Montecitorio as, with a stroke of genius, in 1871, the newly unified government chose it as the site for the Chamber of Deputies. The only place that seemed suitable to hold the assembly room was the courtyard, which was thus covered by one Ingegner Comotto, who, for the seats, designed a wrought-iron structure. Never was there a more precarious and inhospitable structure for the parliamentarians who, it seems, had to keep their hats on their heads to protect them from the summer heat. In 1902 the Chamber turns to the genius of the architect Ernesto Basile, who intervenes heavily on the entire structure. In fact, Basile left only Bernini's façade intact, while all the rest was transformed in accordance with the new Liberty style and with a bit of rhetoric. With new marbles on the floors, decorative and designer details that respected functionality and aesthetic, Montecitorio became an avant-garde building both in terms of technique and style.

The famous "transatlantic", for example, where the parliamentarians take breaks between sittings, owes its name to the ceiling light Basile chose. It really does seem like being on a ship. Much more rigorous and demanding is the language of painter Aristide Sartorio, who dreamt up the enormous decoration in the high part of the hall: a series of figures representing "Italian Civilization, the virtue of the Italian People and the most noteworthy periods from its historical events". To have it adhere perfectly to the curvature of the wall, the artist first painted on paper and then in the second stage applied it to the wall.

Basile would create a new square plan building behind Bernini's. The new façade, that faces onto Piazza del Parlamento, is the best example of the dominant style in the first years of the century. Not the avant-garde anti-conformist one, but the institutional style, where the figures always seem to conceal a certain pride, taking on unsettling positions and, above all, seeming to be animated versions of certain rigid ancient sculptures. Amongst the numerous rooms in Montecitorio, perhaps the most curious is the one recently named after Aldo Moro: it is yellow and enormous, and is decorated with furniture coming from the Royal Palace of Caserta.

27 Villa Paolina
where the royal army conquered Papal Rome

For the visit
Via Piave, 23
Today Villa Paolina is the residence of the French Ambassador to the Holy See.
To visit, it is best to present yourself as a part of a cultural Association. Even if you are on your own, no harm in trying. call 06 42030900
or write a fax to 06 42030968. Own guide.
Free entrance.

When we talk about the Risorgimento, one of the events that springs immediately to mind is the "breaching of Porta Pia", signalling the conquest of Rome by the Piedmontese army. Few know, however, that for Garibaldi's soldiers to enter the city, they had to pass through the garden of a private villa that bordered the ancient walls of the city at Porta Pia. On the 20th September 1870, the French Zouaves, who were defending the Pope, climbed up to the lodge at Villa Paolina and hid among the trees in the park to attack the enemy who had broken through Rome's defensive lines. Their resistance was short lived, as after only twenty minutes Major de Troussures raised a white flag on the roof of the Villa. At that time, the residence belonged to Carlo Bonaparte, the last in the line of the Roman branch of the family, who had left the property in a state of abandon. Long gone are the days when his great-aunt Paolina Borghese, from whom the Villa takes its name, gave her famous receptions here.

The fate of this place seems to be linked to extraordinary women, who made it legendary throughout the 19th century. The first, to be precise, is the sister of Napoleon Bonaparte, who in 1816 acquired it from the Sciarra family, when she decided to withdraw to Rome after the downfall of her brother, the Emperor.

It is love at first sight between the Lady and the

Villa, as the building resembled one of the most elegant "country" residences of the period. The character conferred to the place by Cardinal Silvio Valenti Gonzaga can still be felt. He was the Secretary of State to Pope Benedict XIV, and had acquired the land in 1748. There is an exceptional document which establishes the date of the project: in a huge painting by Gian Paolo Pannini (famous for his highly detailed reconstructions of galleries and similar scenes) from 1749, paintings from the Valenti collection are represented, amongst which can be seen the plan for the Villa Paolina Lodge (Vodret). As testified to by other scenes from the 18th century, its structure today is exactly as it was originally. Only the garden, which at the time was Italian style, has undergone modifications and was reduced to leave space for post-unification building speculation. Inside you can still breathe the refined and cultured atmosphere that the Lady wanted to create here. While the stuccoes on the ground floor refer to antique-style models, as was typical of the antiquarian taste of the 18th century, the 19th century rooms display a more romantic nature. In one room there are landscapes of the Nile and Egyptian temples, in memory of the Napoleonic campaigns, while the salon on the first floor is decorated in a grisaille style, however, the most fascinating room surely has to be the Sala delle Muse (Room of the Muses). An homage to femininity could not have been missing from the home of the Lady who, upon arrival in Rome from Paris, surrounded herself with the most fashionable artists and invited Antonio Canova, the most well-known sculptor of the time, to do a portrait of her as Venus. At the centre of the ceiling there is Minerva surrounded by the Muses, while in the lunettes famous women from antiquity are placed: Sappho, Aspasia and Corinna. A line up missing only Paolina. Madame Mère's veto for attributing the name Villa Bonaparte fell on deaf ears. The choice to only use the owner's first name increased the place's fame and rendered this small corner of peace even more legendary.

28 Villino Douhet
where the aviator with a passion for art lived

For the visit
Via Marcantonio Colonna, 23
To arrange a visit you need to call 063215145 (ext. 105) and then send an official request to Presidente Nazionale dell'Associazione Arma dell'Aeronautica Via M. Colonna, 23 00192 Roma.

Often a visit to a private home serves not only to discover the history, but also the human events of the place. This is what happens on entering Villino Douhet, which the Italian airforce dedicated to the general who devised and decorated it in the 1920s. We are in the part of Prati closest to the river, where amongst the tree-lined streets some of the most interesting Liberty-style villas can be found hiding. The building in question doesn't have any particular exterior decoration. Actually, it looks rather severe and simple, but inside, another world is revealed. The world which captivated Giulio Douhet, art lover an expert aviator. His role in the army is above all noted for his celebrated "theory of dominion in the air", still much discussed in the military field. His house almost seems to be an efficient refuge, a place to take a moment away from the military tasks and dedicate yourself to a much more intimate world. This is shown by the fact that, it seems, Douhet himself has done some of the decoration in the Villa. Following the tastes of the time, the walls and flooring show some of history's most famous works of art, put next to each other with an exceptional freedom and no care for any temporal cohesion.

Under Gothic arches, invariably decorated with cornicing and starry belts, you pass from a reproduction of a Byzantine *Madonna and child* to Botticelli's *Calumny* and finally to the *Medusa*. Despite the somber tones and a certain severity to the villa as a whole, the apartment is clear proof of a refined taste, coherent with what, for example, Coppedè was applying in the construction of the residential area of the Palazzi degli Ambasciatori in the Salario district. The style entered history with the name of eclecticism, but maybe it would be more correct, in Douhet's case, to call it a free flying through the history of art.

29 Villa Aurelia
where American Academy holds its prestigious events

For the visit
Largo di Porta San Pancrazio, 1
To arrange a visit you need to contact the Accademia Americana on 06 5846408.
Guide service available.
Entrance fee.

Today this is one of the most sought-after locations for receptions and gala dinners and recent theatre for worldly political events. Above all however, Villa Aurelia is one of the spots from where you can enjoy one the best panoramas of Rome, higher than the terrace at the Gianicolo. We are a stone's throw from Porta San Pancrazio, where in the 3rd century A.D. the Aurelian walls were clambering up. It seems that on this spot, a defensive tower stood, which in the 17th century was reduced to ruins. On this is based the building realized by Cardinal Gerolamo Farnese between 1650 and 1667, not far from a house commissioned by Alessandro Farnese, before he became Pope Paul III, and which was destroyed during the Roman Republic of 1849. Initially, the Cardinal had in mind more the construction of a loggia, to go with the surrounding park and take advantage of the westerly breeze. Soon the project was transformed, however, into an actual two-storey Villa, with rooms and salons, a gallery for the works of art and a spiral staircase, which still leads to a loggia facing a breathtaking view of Rome. An inventory from the time described accurately the furniture, the works of art, stucco decorations and the grotesques which today have all but disappeared. Changes of ownership into irresponsible hands and, above all, unforeseen events during wars at the end of the 19th century heavily damage the Villa, which would then be rebuilt in the 1950s respecting the standards of the original structure.

In fact, from the middle of the 18th century the residence underwent a frantic change in ownership: from the Farnese it passed onto the Bourbons, who then rented it to Count Ferdinando Giraud. His heirs managed to grab it up for a ridiculous sum and sold it to Count Alessandro Savorelli. It was he who transferred his candle making factory here (there is still one of the same name at Forlì) and called upon the architect Virginio Vespignani to redo the building. A task that was interrupted with the occupation by Garibaldi's troops in 1849 and the following destruction of the roof and the south facing façade. Falling into disrepair, Savorelli had to leave the property to Monte di Pietà, from whom it was brought, in 1885, by Mrs. Clara Jessup Heyland, who had decided to relocate to a quiet spot to live with her husband, invalided from the war. From Mrs. Heyland, Villa Aurelia passed to the American Academy, which still manages it today, and above all, keeps it like a small jewel, both inside and in the garden. Walking around here in Spring is a true delight, thanks to the pines, the perfectly mown lawn and the peaceful corners, like the secret garden with a fountain hidden amidst luxurious vegetation.

30 Palazzo Madama
where Austria became an ostrich

For the visit
Piazza Madama
The Senate opens up to the public the first Saturday of every month. However, it is possible to request special visits on other days by calling
06 67062430
or sending a fax to
06 67063513
or an e-mail to
visitealsenato@senato.it.
It is easier to obtain permission if the request comes from a cultural association.
Guide service available.
Free entrance.

In Rome there is a very popular term they call the police. When they want to identify it clearly and slightly ironically, they call it "la madama", to underline its austere character and irrefutable decisions. This curious name has its origins rooted in antiquity: apparently it was coined in the 18th century, when the headquarters of the police was transferred by Pope Benedict XIV to Palazzo Madama. It is incredible to think that today it still holds memories of their rather short stay. In fact, only forty years later, the police forces are replaced by the central office for Rome's first republican experiment (1798-1799), sparked by the French Revolution, while in the mid-19th century Pius IX transferred there the Ministry of Finance and the extraction for the lottery, which before took place in Montecitorio. The public offices adapted, to their new functions, the rooms of what had until then been a patrician residence, developed over the course of three centuries of changes in ownership. The first nucleus of the Palace dates back to the 15th century, when France acquired land from the Abbey at Farfa in order to build lodgings for the pilgrims from Via Francigena (the pilgrimage route between Canterbury and Rome). A short-lived project, as after only a few years it passes to the Medici, forced to find refuge in Rome from Florence.
It was here that a part of Lorenzo the Magnificent's celebrated library was placed, recreating

the atmosphere of the Florentine court, first thanks to Cardinal Giovanni de' Medici (the future Pope Leo X), then to his cousin, Giuliano, and finally to Margaret of Austria, wife of Alessandro de' Medici. She is the Madama from whom the Palace takes its name. One of the main rooms of the building was decorated in her honour, where a wooden paneled ceiling with gilt stuccoes hosts a relief of an ostrich. According to some art historians, the choice of such a singular animal would have been linked to a jocular play on words between *Autriche* (Austria in French) and *autruche* (ostrich in French), even if it is far more probable that the exotic animal is more of a symbol of speed and strength. Apart from this exemplary work of craftsmanship, not much remains of the 17th century pictorial decoration. Excluding the tapestries dedicated to the story of *Tobias and the Angel*, in the Sala della Firma (Signature Room), as well as the frieze painted by Pietro Paolo Baldini with the stories of Pope Pius IV, all the rest dates back to the 18th century and, above all, to the era of the Risorgimento. It was in fact in this period that the building was chosen as the seat of the Senate of the Republic. There is an oddity regarding the fresco painted by Giovanni Paolo Pannini, which decorates the room where Presidential meetings take place: this beautiful painted architecture, which culminates in the chariot of the Sun, was originally to be found at Palazzo Bachetoni in via del Tritone. When, in 1926, it was decided that the building would be demolished the fresco was salvaged and placed in Palazzo Madama. Possibly the most representative room in the Palace, after the assembly hall, is the Sala Maccari, which takes its name from the artist who decorated it in 1880, following a call for tenders by the Ministry of Education, which at that time also carried out the functions of the Ministry for Cultural Heritage. We have here a collection of scenes and symbols that hark back to the ancient Roman Senate: on one wall Cicero is shown in his harangue against Catiline, who on the extreme opposite side is listening to him, grim-faced and isolated from the rest of the assembly. On another wall the old Appio Claudio the censor is being led into the presence of the Senators to convince them to not accept the humiliating terms of peace imposed on them by Pyrrhus, whilst Marco Papirio is motionless on hearing of the invasion of the Gauls. Everything is dominated by four medallions dedicated to commerce and the arts. A beautiful homage to ancient moral integrity and the productive activities, devised to exhort the new inhabitants of Palazzo Madama towards virtuous and informed acts with respect to the responsibilities they have been trusted with by the electorate. Who knows how much today the Senators taking a break or reading the newspapers in this room actually look at these paintings…

31 Istituto Nazionale di Studi Romani
where the Temple of Diana is hidden, perhaps

For the visit
Piazza dei Cavalieri di Malta, 2
Visits to the Institute are advisable on workdays and in the morning, when the offices are open. To arrange a date call 06 5743442 or send a fax to 06 5743447.
Own guide.
Free entrance.

The home of the Istituto Nazionale di Studi Romani is well-known above all by archaeology and ancient history scholars, who have the privilege of being able to regularly enter one of the most fascinating spots in Rome, serenely perched on the Aventine Hill, where it enjoys an extraordinary view of the city. The hill is so elevated that from up there you can't even hear the chaos of the traffic along the Tiber. It was not by chance that it was chosen for the site of a convent for the nuns devoted to Saints Bonifacio and Alessio, who took care of, amongst other things, the church right next door to the convent. The Institute is very old and was founded in the 7th century. The structure was probably erected on the ruins of the old Temple of Diana, an enormous piece of architecture in which, it is held, Gaius Gracchus sought refuge in 122 B.C. The discovery, for now actually only a hypothesis, was published by the archaeologist Laura Vendittelli in 2007, on the basis of a close examination of the *Forma Urbis*, a faithful plan of Ancient Rome, unfortunately in fragments. Whilst waiting for the results of eventual excavations to be carried out in the courtyard (but there are no funds), the visit offers the chance to walk inside the 16th century cloisters, realized through the use of marble and ancient granite columns, all different, even their capitals.

After crossing the garden which takes you to the panoramic terrace, you can gain access to the interior, where you can admire the remaining decorations, which are few but valuable. In the room where the nuns have placed their library, a fresco with a subject typical of the Enlightenment was painted in the 18th century: the *Allegory of the progress of the Sciences and the Arts*, dated 1754. The rest of the main floor was inhabited by Carlo IV of the Bourbons, who chose here to spend his exile after due to Napoleon's conquest of Spain. His rooms boast polychrome marble flooring and Pompeian style frescoes on the walls. It is the perfect setting for the Institute, being a place for delving deeper into the literature and the history of Ancient Rome and where, the most deserving, are able to take part in the *Certamen Capitolinum*, a prestigious recognition for researchers and archaeologists.

32 Casa dei Cavalieri di Rodi

where the best views of the Fori Imperiali can be enjoyed

For the visit
Piazza del Grillo, 1
Visits regularly take place on Tuesday and Thursday mornings thanks to an agreement between the Sovereign Military Order of Malta and the Council of Rome. Bookings can therefore be made calling 060608.
To visit the Casa on other days, a pass can be requested directly from ACISMOM by calling 06 6796384, but it is not easy to obtain.
Own guide.
Entrance fee.

There was a moment in the history of Rome where anything was possible, even that a group of monks would take over the building of the Temple of Augustus' Forum, creating the Monastery of St. Basil. It was the 9th century A.D. and for too long now the cardinal spots of Imperial Rome had lost their roles, and above all, their dignity. Even the most imposing temples, such as the one dedicated by Augustus to Mars Ultor could be "desecrated" and turned into new places of worship: and so the apse becomes the church and the forecourt the convent. The new seat would have made use of the imposing wall made of fire-resistant rock that the Emperor had erected to protect the Forum from the frequent fires in the Subarra district. It is probable that the three ancient columns still standing have survived thanks to the Basilian monastery, which held out there until the 19th century, when it was demolished causing protests from artists and intellectuals. A few centuries after the arrival of the Basilian monks, at the beginning of the 13th century, the Knights of St. John of Jerusalem, known also as the Knights of Rhodes, came to Rome, escaping from the Turkish invasion of the Holy Land. Arriving in a city where the ancient ruins are up for anyone's grabs, they decided to build their own place putting it upon one of the exedras in the Forum of Augustus. Shortly after, talk of the monks of St. Basil died away, but it is known for certain that the Knights kept the spirit of the Saint alive, so much so that when they decided to move to the Aventine (that area of the Forum was a mire), they dedicated

their main altar to St. Basil and not to their protector St. John the Baptist (see Santa Maria del Priorato, p.135).

The structure remained almost abandoned until 1466, when Pope Paul II nominates his grandson, Marco Barbo, as administrator of the Priory of the Knights of Rhodes. It was he to commission the works that gave the Casa the look it has today. Some of the Venetian details give rise to the belief that the Cardinal, who was Cardinal of San Marco, used some of the workers at that time working on that construction of Palazzo Venezia. In those years the seat of the Knights returned to Augustus' Forum and on the outside wall appear the coats of arms, of Papa Barbo and the gothic-like mullioned window, still visible today. Through a steep staircase you reach the Salone d'Onore (Room of Honour) where the Knights used to meet. An opening in the wall allowed the Priory to call their attention from above. We find here the flags of the eight languages of the Order of Malta (Provence, Auvergne, France, Italy, Aragon, England, Germany and Castile) and two geographical maps showing where the Knights were present in antiquity. From here you pass to the so-called Sala della Loggetta, created by closing the atrium of an ancient Roman house (the atrium became, on the floor below, the Church of St. John the Baptist). In the room, where the wall of the Forum is clearly visible, the reconstruction of a clypeus with the head of Jupiter Ammon and two caryatids is exhibited, fruit of the works following the excavation in the zone carried out in the 15th century. The fresco with a *Crucifix between the Madonna and*

St. John dates back to the following century and is attributed to Sebastiano del Piombo. The painting is one of the few remaining traces from the Nunnery of the Annunciation which occupied the structure in the 16th century, when the Knights moved again to the Aventine Hill (the nuns were charged with the task of converting young Jewish women). The last part of the visit is possibly the most exhilarating one, as it takes you, through the internal stairway, to the Loggia which faces over the Imperial Fora. It is one of the favourite places amongst the tourists strolling between Piazza Venezia and the Coliseum. Only when you are on the terrace do you discover that the walls are completely frescoed by painters from the Mantegna circle. Inside of a false architecture landscapes with animals, exotic birds and pruned topiary trees appear. On the pedestals you can see the coat of arms of Cardinal Barbo, while on the cornicing portraits of the Emperors are found. It is one of the most elegant settings, testimony to the transition from medieval culture to that of the Renaissance, which in Rome is rare to find (see also the Casina del Cardinal Bessarione - the house of Cardinal Bessarione -, p. 99). Further proof of this phenomenon are the Byzantine arches and the round arches found within the same structure, a sign that architecture was undergoing a delicate period of transition.

33 Vatican Gardens
where the Pope used to go hunting

For the visit

Viale Vaticano (Vatican Museum entrance)
The Vatican Museums organize booked group visits: www.museivaticani.va Bookings can be made calling 06 69884676 or 06 69883145. Guide service available. Entrance fee. Inside the gardens you can find the Casino of Pope Pius IV which has been entrusted to the Papal Academy of Sciences: visits are permitted only to a few cultural associations, but you can have a go calling 06 69883195, it doesn't cost anything. Good luck!

This is one of the most fascinating and secret places in Rome, where over eight centuries' worth of extraordinary monuments are held. Today only a small part of the Vatican Gardens are open to the public: they occupy over half of the entire Vatican State. It is not widely known that next to the house that Pope Pius IV had built, and which takes his name, there is exceptional botanical garden, entrusted in 1564 to Michele Mercati. This expert wrote to all the papal nuncios in Europe (the Pope's Ambassadors) to have them send plants and trees that were not found in Italy. He even entertained relations with King Philip II of Spain, who sent him a Nicotiana (tobacco plant), marigolds and pepper plants. Mercati's legacy was taken over in the 17th century by Johannes Faber who continued to import exotic plants from all over the world. It was in this period that bananas came to the Vatican. By then, the gardens were for the most part a great orchard, handy for the growing of fruit and vegetables. It was only over the last few decades that the rural part of the garden was greatly reduced in size, leaving only a small part where nuns of the order of St. Clare grow the vegetables destined for the Pope's plate. In the higher part of the garden, where today there is still a wood, hunts used to be organized, led by the

Pope. Every year the King of Naples donated pheasants to the Holy Father's hunts, to be caught and served at the court banquets.

In the 17th century, an incredible fifteen hundred finches arrived from Lombardy. Leo XIII was one of the most avid hunters, to which he dedicated himself from a "roccolo" (a small construction for birds surrounded by trees), placed high up hidden among the trees, which can still be seen.

The popes have always invested a lot in the decoration of this spot, even if it was destined to be seen by only a few people. It wasn't really an instrument for propaganda, as the other works carried out in the city. The reason behind the great interest in this place is linked to the significance that the Vatican Gardens had assumed over time. In the mid-13th century, when they were created by Pope Nicolas II, this park was filled with symbolic value: it was the hortus conclusus (enclosed garden) of the Virgin, evoked by the presence of roses and lilies, which in the Song of Songs refer to the Madonna. Thereafter, each Pope left his mark, enriching it time after time both with architectural elements and botanical wonders. One of the most beautiful monuments is the Fontana della Galera (galley) commissioned by Pope Paul V Borghese. A true papal vessel reproduced with various entwining metals ranging from copper to bronze, suspended on the water. Matteo Barberini, the future Pope Urban V, dedicated to the fountain these lines: «the popes' cannons do not shoot fire, but holy water».

To discover even the most inaccessible corners, it could prove useful reading the recently published book by Dr. Alberta Campitelli, in charge of the Parks and Historic Villas in the City of Rome. (Jaca Book).

34 Casino Borghese
where you can discover masterpieces hidden in the storage rooms

For the visit
Giardini di Villa Borghese (entrance from Via Pinciana)
Visits to the storage rooms can be booked using the same service as that for the Galleria Borghese. Call n. 06 32810. Guide service available. Entrance fee.

The Borghese Gallery is said to be "the most beautiful museum in the world", above all since history has left it intact over time. The relationship between the works of art and the setting is the same as it has been for over two centuries and the collection has not once forsaken any fundamental painting or sculpture. The museum set-up in 1998 determined the need to select the masterpieces to be put on show for the public, which gather here every day in huge numbers from all over the world to admire Bernini, Caravaggio, Titian, Raphael and Canova. Not everything made it to the final official selection on show. There are an amazing 263 paintings, 19 bronzes, 7 small ancient marble statues and a clock dating back to the time of Cardinal Scipione Borghese conserved on the second floor of the Casino, right underneath the roof. The atmosphere here is very different from the rest of the museum, as in the storage rooms the works are displayed on the entire surface of the walls up to a height which makes it impossible to see the details, as was the norm in the 17th- century dwellings. Amongst these hidden treasures it is worth noting the Venus by Baldassarre Peruzzi, Christ Carrying the Cross by Sebastiano del Piombo and the Sacred Family by Scipione Pulzone. Standing out amongst the paintings from the 17th century are St.Francis by Hannibal Carracci, the Mendicante by Ribera, Susanna and the Elders by Honthorst, or the great painting by Lavinia Fontana showing Minerva in the act of getting dressed.

One curiosity in this collection, which by no means is to be considered of secondary importance, are the works in small format, such as battle scene of the *Taking of Jerusalem*, painted by Antonio Tempesta or the small landscapes by Paul Bril. These are examples of a refined taste which often were found hanging in the more intimate rooms of the old residence and destined to amaze only the most privileged of guests. Just like today.

35 Palazzo della Consulta

where the Pope invested the Lottery funds

For the visit
Piazza del Quirinale, 41
For a visit you need to contact the Constitutional Court on 06 46981.
Groups belonging to cultural associations gain access more easily.
Own guide. Free entrance.

You don't always think of the fact that the Popes had the duty of organizing efficiently Roman life and its administration. They weren't simple Lords, who enjoyed the privileges of court life and the respect of the international community, but true governors who had to manage the daily life of thousands of people, citizens and visitors passing through. Administrative necessities often determined urban layout and the construction of new buildings. Julius II, in the 16th century, tried to create an administrative zone, opening up the axis of via Giulia, but its close proximity to the Tiber immediately put the stability of the buildings at risk. Over two centuries later, Pope Clement XII tried his hand at creating a seat for the papal tribunals on the Quirinal Hill and invited, in 1732, the architect Ferdinando Fuga (the same who would arrange the Scuderie (mews) and the entire Piazza) to make use of the structure of the Baths of Constantine, which were thus raised to the ground and used as foundations. His is the very Classical project of Palazzo della Consulta, an enormous construction which on its façade reveals the tripartite organization on the interior. With the money gathered from the Lottery, the Pope gives a new home to the Tribunal of the Sacred Council, to the Segnatura of the Brevi and three military companies.

The Palace immediately takes on a symbolic value, so much so that Mazzini established his general quarters there during the Roman Republic of 1849. After various ministerial designation (Foreign Office, Colonies), in 1955 it became the seat of the Constitutional Court. The tympanum the surmounts the entrance is decorated with the figures of Justice and Religion, the two cornerstones of the work of the Tribunal. Their position is a clear homage to the Day and Night that Michelangelo placed on the tomb of the Medicis in Florence. The decoration inside was inspired by the style and the themes of Neoclassical culture. On the ceilings bas-reliefs alternate with mythological figures, such as *Hercules and Cybele, Proserpina and Vigilance*, and the frescoes where Ceres asks Jupiter to free her daughter Proserpina, kidnapped by Pluto. The route, which touches on the antechambers, offices and salons, offers the chance to come into contact with a taste in transition between the classical nostalgia of the 18th century and the rhetoric of 19th century officialdom.

36 Casina of Cardinal Bessarione
where medieval Rome is over

For the visit
Via di Porta San Sebastiano, 9
Request for visits must be made to the Sovraintendenza Comunale on 06 67103238.

It is curious to think just how some places in Rome got their names. Very often, Palaces, residences or small fragments from antiquity are known by names that were born over time, through word of mouth and not thanks to written documents of inscriptions. Today it is not always easy to go back to the origins of the reasons for these names, but it can be interesting to try and reconstruct the path of the tradition and try to find a plausible explanation. With the Casina of Cardinal Bessarione, we find ourselves facing exactly one of these enigmatic cases, as it seems (today it is practically certain) that the Cardinal never actually lived in this "country" house, built in the first half of the 15th century on via Appia, among the most ancient tombs in Rome which date back to the 3rd century B.C., before the Aurelian Walls were erected in the 2nd century A.D. and the necropolis was moved even further from the city centre. Well, we don't know precisely why the Cardinal was associated with this place - maybe the connection derives from the fact that the structure was reserved for the bishop of Tusculum, a duty that Bessarione had taken on between 1449 and 1468, or maybe because Bessarione owned some vineyards between San Sisto and San Cesareo, right in the area where the house is found.

This strong doubt emerges from the fact that in all the decorations of the house, the Cardinal's coat of arms does not appear once, whilst that of Cardinal Battista Zeno is often found. He too was Bishop of Tusculum more or less in the same period as Bessarione. It could be hypothesized that Zeno carried out some heavy restructuring work on the house, but it is difficult to say with certainty what Bessarione's involvement was, if any. His presence though is evoked through the decorations and the structure of this place. As in the case of the House of the Knights of Rhodes (see p. 89), here we are again confronted with an example of architecture that marks the transition between a Medieval house and a Renaissance residence. Between the 14th and the 15th century a transformation in the mentality and daily habits in Europe, and in particular in Rome, was seen. Just think about the fact that the Casina originally had a tower, today no longer in existence, and a loggia. These two elements allow us to understand how architecture reflects a turning point of an era. The tower in the 14th century was the typical building on the rise in Rome after the fall of the Empire, useful for protecting its inhabitants from disorderly citizens in the absence of a strong regime to offer control. The loggia, which created a connection between the interior and the urban context, was invented in the 15th century, an age characterized by great geographical discoveries, when new cultural openness was in the air, which was also expressed in the structure of the dwellings, thanks also to the loggias which opened out to the outside. The peculiarity of the Bessarione loggia is that the internal decoration, that has as its theme the countryside, seems to merge into the bucolic landscape which was revealed beyond the arches, as if the real architecture was continued inside the painted one. The reference to the internal courtyards of a Roman *domus*, where on the walls mythological perspectives and scenes were to be found, is obvious. With the return of piece to Rome and the recognition of the universal authority of the Pope, the people in the city began to reason more serenely when it came to architecture and began to gather new cultural inspiration arriving from the rest of the peninsula. Bessarione, originally from Trabzon (Turkey), was educated in Greece and always maintained a close relationship with Venice. He was a cosmopolitan man, one of the first intellectuals to unite in himself a passion for scholarly and aesthetic culture with an interest for natural sciences and platonic philosophy. He was one of those personalities who showed how religious education and dogma, which had dominated the medieval mind, had given way to a dialogue between theology and Classical culture. The images we find drawn on the walls of the Casina represent the beginning of this dialogue, which, over a period of two hundred years would evolve into the complex decorative cycles in Villa Farnesina or the numerous noble residences in Italy, where a return to certain antique ways happens. Even if the Cardinal had never lived here, the decorative themes do reflect his culture. At the time of Bessarione, the grotesques had not yet been discovered: the natural elements which cover the walls of the rooms do not correspond to each other, they are all a bit different. The animals shown, such as a small snake with ears appearing in the Sala Regia, have no relationship between them. Above all, what stands out is the complete absence of symmetry. To understand the sense behind this decoration, one of the fundamental texts comes to our aid, which contributed to the new repertory of the Humanist artists: the *Hypnerotomachia Poliphili*, attributed to Francesco Colonna. From this mysterious and not perfectly deciphered 14th-century work, very popular in its time, come the fountains from which flowers are blooming and a series of images, all unconnected, that we can also find at the Casina. The decorations go from the basement, where the Cardinal probably used to dine in order to escape from the summer heat, to the floors above (at the time only connected by an external staircase). The themes in the *cubiculum*, the old bedroom, are curious: rich with open pomegranates (the Passion of Christ), just as is the presence of a lunette with a saint standing on a dragon in the Sala Regia. It is probably one of the frescoes that would have been on the outside of the building in the original 14th-century structure, engulfed in the expansionary works of the following century.

37. Villino Hüffer
where intellectuals took part to memorable receptions

For the visit
Via Nazionale, 191
The Villino holds the Bank of Italy's Historical Archive. The body allows access to scholars and groups from cultural associations. You need to attach the association's by-laws to the visit request.
Call 0647925930.
Own guide.
Free entrance.

The decision to move the capital of the new Kingdom of Italy to Rome unleashed a building frenzy in the city, the likes of which hadn't been seen since the time of Pope Julius II. With the opening of via Nazionale, thanks to the dedication of Count de Mérode, the area between the Quirinal and Termini Station was transformed into an enormous open-air work site. Over a period of less than twenty years, public buildings and private residences sprang up at an extraordinary rate, all having in common the style of the time, called "Neo-Renaissance". Villino Hüffer was no exception, built by the German Baron, Wilhelm Hüffer, between 1880 and 1883. It took only three years to bring to fruition his real estate investment from his monies garnered in the textile industry, which allowed him entry into the Roman noble society circles, now open to bourgeois entrepreneurs. The new villino is the key that opened the doors for him to the Capital's high society.

The receptions that the Hüffers gave in their residence were famous and also happened to be frequented by Gabriele D'Annunzio. Today as it was then, the Bank of Italy conserves the building in impeccable order, from the wrought-iron canopy, reminiscent early 20th-century Paris, to the polychrome marbles, stuccoes and the wall paintings decorating the interior. Hüffer definitely spared no expense.

For the visit
Via Nazionale, 91
Visits to Palazzo Koch are permitted to groups who make a request through a cultural association. There is no fixed calendar and visits can be arranged calling 0647923012
or sending a fax to 0647922983 to the attention of Servizio Segretariato Generale and to the Servizio Segreteria Particolare.
Guide service available.
Free entrance.

38 Palazzo Koch
where Italy's gold reserve is stored

It took four years, between 1888 and 1892, to build one of the most majestic buildings in modern Rome. One of the secrets of its fast construction was perhaps the fact that marble from Tivoli was used only on the façade (punctuated by the three Classical orders: Doric, Ionic and Corinthian), while the rest of the external structure was done in stucco, modeled with such skill that it looks like travertine marble.

Its author was Gaetano Koch, who won the tender from the Bank of Italy because he managed to devise a project that was both functional and representative at the same time. It suffices to think that the building has five floors, two of which are underground: it is here that Italy's gold reserve is kept, guaranteeing the financial stability of the country. At one time it was possible to gain access to the building through two entrances on via Nazionale, one leading to the desks open to the public, the other to the offices. When the Bank of Italy closed its branches to become an administrative body, one of the two entrances was closed. Today the only entrance leads to the Cortile d'Onore (Courtyard of Honour) where a bust of Koch is on displayand, at the end of a gallery, you can spot the ancient statue of Antinous which was found whilst digging the building's foundations. Upon entering the building, you go up to the first floor along the Scalone d'Onore, which seems almost to be suspended in mid air, jutting out from the wall without any support. The 3rd century A.D. Hellenistic-style sarcophagus at its feet is extraordinary.

On the main floor we find a series of rooms where the pieces of the Bank of Italy's collection are exhibited. Almost all of them came from clients' collections, who, to pay off some of their debt, ceded some of their assets to the bank. In the centre of the Sala delle Tartarughe (Tortoise Room), you can see a reproduction of the celebrated fountain in Piazza Mattei, whilst in the Corridoio of archaeological exhibits you can see the *Tabula Peutingeriana* (Peutinger Map). Despite being a copy from 1753, this map is an extraordinary document, as it shows the military roads from the Roman Empire, traced probably from an old design by Marcus Vipsanius Agrippa, Emperor Augustus' son-in-law. It is almost seven metres long and shows the stages of the routes without bothering to show the distances. Following on from the Salon di San Marco, so called because of the presence of a print from the Venetian basilica, and the Salone di Pelle (leather), from the material on the seats, we arrive in the Saletta Cinese where you can see some works that belonged to Riccardo Gualino (1879 – 1964), a rich patron from Biella. You pass by Persian peacocks in gold and silver, to the heads of Khmer Buddhas, to the Indian statues and Chinese vases which range from 1000 years B.C. to 1900 A.D. Modern art is present too, represented by a lovely collection of paintings by Filippo de Pisis.

Crossing these rooms always stirs up strange emotions, even if they don't hold masterpieces: at one time national financial policy was decided here (the value of our money), today it is monitored that our finances don't get out of control, under pressure from the current international crisis.

39 Palazzo Vidoni Caffarelli
where an old Roman calendar was saved

For the visit

Corso Vittorio Emanuele II, 116
Gaining entrance to Vidoni-Caffarelli has become more difficult recently as the Department has less funds to dedicate to overtime pay for the guards who have to be there during opening hours. Requests, in any case, should be forwarded on the headed paper of a cultural association to: Presidenza del Consiglio dei Ministri- Dipartimento Funzione pubblica-Ufficio Affari Generali e del Personale, Corso Vittorio Emanuele, 116 - 00186 Roma. For further information call 06 689971
Own guide.
Free entrance.

The origins of this large Palace that overlooks corso Vittorio Emanuele and which one whizzes by every day without noticing it, go back to the 16th century. Yet it is a small treasure chest, currently home to the offices of the Department of Public Administration, the reason why it has been so well conserved and also why it is so difficult to visit. It was erected in 1515, at the wish of Bernardino Caffarelli, who enlarged the family property close to the ruins of Domitian's Stadium. The project was commissioned to a pupil of Raphael's. Contrary to popular belief, the main façade is situated on via del Sudario, a choice that in the 19th century was not approved of by the new owner. As a matter of fact, Duke Carlo Giovanni Bandini appointed the architect Settimj to design a new façade on corso Vittorio Emanuele, to integrate the two fronts and to redistribute the rooms inside. Having climbed up the 19th century staircase, you enter the Sala Carlo V (today the Minister's office) where the most precious frescoes are held, the work of Perin del Vaga: episodes from the life of Charles V are depicted, who is supposed to have met Pope Paul III here, alternating with portraits of Roman and German emperors. The adjacent room represents a jump forward of two hundred years in time, to a setting covered with mirrors decorated with gilt frames in the pure Rococo style.

The Duchess Bandini asked for it, who also chose the sea-green colour and, at the centre of the ceiling, a representation of a Cupid armed with arrows. La Sala delle Udience (Audience room), today the office of the Head of the Cabinet, shows on the ceiling three 18th-century oval canvases with the allegory of the arts. On the opposite side of the Palazzo, one of the most refined room opens up, called the Sala del Biliardo, where the frieze painted by the Zuccari brothers narrates the stories of Tobias. Upon close look, we can see that the wood-panel ceiling has a cornicing covered in pure gold. On the second floor there are two important rooms. In the Sala dei Fasti Prenesti, Cardinal Stoppani, in 1774, looked after the marble tablets from the calendar of Vallerio Flacca thus ensuring they were not dispersed forever (today they are held in the Museo Nazionale Romano). For a long time however, it was wrongly thought that this room used to be the ancient chapel. Next to it is the Sala Pomepiana, a room that couldn't have been left out of an 18th century palace, above all after the discovery of the ruins at Pompeii, which turned the grotesque decorations on a red background into something extremely fashionable.

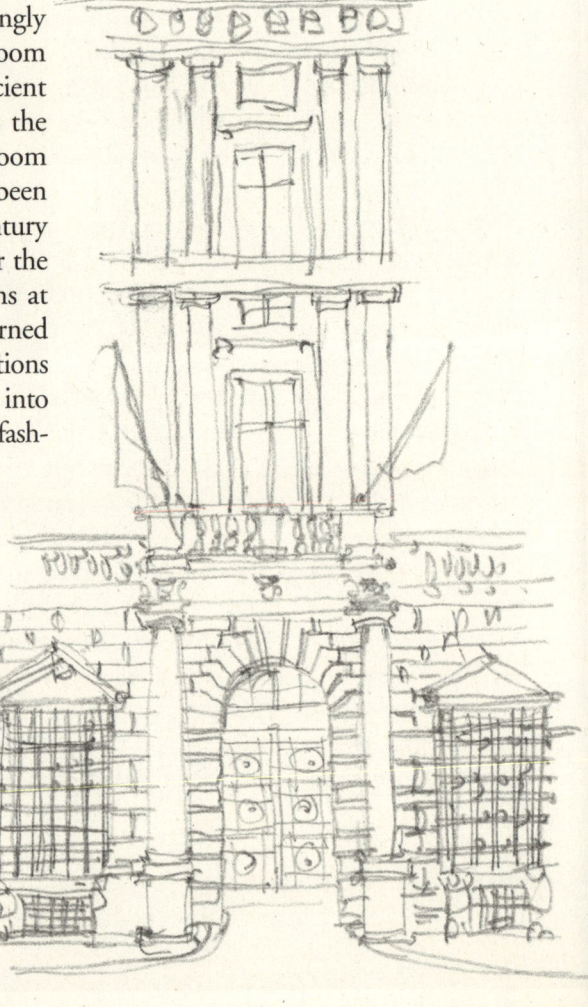

CONVENTS
CHURCHES
LIBRARIES

40 Convent of Trinità dei Monti

where a painted sundial shows the times around the world

For the visit
Piazza della Trinità dei Monti
Recently the Sisters of the Sacred Heart, now few and old, left the convent to the Monastic Brotherhood of Jerusalem, who offer guided visits open to everybody on Tuesdays at 10:15 and Sundays at 9:15. All you need to do is turn up at the entrance of the monastery at the top of the staircase on the left of the church. Organized groups can request a visit with their own guide or ask if the nuns are available. The nun in charge of the visits receives requests via fax on 0669941646. Fast response.
For further information call 066794179.
Guide service available. Free entry, donations are welcome.

One of the oldest French settlements in Rome was thanks to an Italian. In the 15th century, King Louis XI of France heard of Francesco da Paola's extreme decision to withdraw into a solitary hermit existence. Despite all this having taken place in Calabria, a territory cut off from all relations with Europe, the news reached Paris and the sovereign, in admiration, invited the monk to settle in France. Francesco da Paola, taking this as a sign of Providence, in 1482 in France, with his dream of one day founding an order and putting down roots in Rome, the heart of Christianity. The chance came a few years later, when King Charles VIII agreed to finance the foundation of a convent and the monk pointed out the slope on Pincio as being a favourable spot for its construction. It was an area of land that had been abandoned for centuries, where in ancient times the of the vineyards of Lucullus were to be found. The fall of the Roman Empire and the sacking by Alaric caused the memory of this noble presence to be forgotten and the entire area was the subject of chance and superficial works by individuals. Such as the Barbaro brothers, who sold the land, for a sum that, all in all, cannot be considered high, to the French Cardinal of Santa Sabina. It was in 1494 when the foundations are laid for what would be one of the most prestigious convents in the city, where scholarly monks would live and a huge library created.

The decorative works on the building dragged on for two centuries and saw the major Mannerist artists working on the chapels of the church and in the spaces around the cloisters. Underneath the portico fresco scenes were painted of the life of San Francesco da Paola and the main one was given to Cavalier d'Arpino (the Canonization, ruined unfortunately during the Roman Republic of 1798). Under the vaults are portraits of all the Kings of France from the Middle Ages to the 17th century. However, it was during the explosion of the Baroque that the convent acquired it most interesting and curious works, which today still render it a unique place in the world. The eclectic culture of the monks, their interest in science in addition to that in the Sacred Scriptures, made them the protagonists of some small but memorable feats. For the decoration of the refectory, the Jesuit brother Andrea Pozzo was called upon, who had distinguished himself for having painted the ceiling in the Church of Sant'Ignazio di Loyola, creating a false cupola through the play of perspectives. The painter offered the same solution on the ceiling at Trinità dei Monti, where he created two medallions that appear to be cracked and covered the entire surface of the refectory walls with a lively scene of the Marriage at Cana. As was typical in 17th-century painting, when art had to above all provoke strong emotions, the painter described the moment when water was turned to wine, causing a surprised reaction among the guests gathered on the left-hand wall and the servants on the right-hand wall. Their bodies are stirred as they pass to each other the news of the miracle behind a balustrade, they are separated by a colonnade in perspective, standing on a floor which seems to be designed as if it were an elongation of the of the real one. Pozza lingers on the addition of important details, such as the light, which floods the walls that are illuminated by the windows and leaves the walls between the windows is semidarkness. Of all the spans, the only one without a balustrade in that at the end of the room, where Jesus and Mary are sitting: the servant who is offering them the jug with water (or is it already wine?) seems ready to come down to pour the contents into the glasses of the monks, seated at the tables in the centre of the room: it seems that they too have been invited to join in this miracle. The choice of this Jesuit artist was not haphazard, because in the convent at Trinità dei Monti, the optical effects of the painting have always been much appreciated. This is

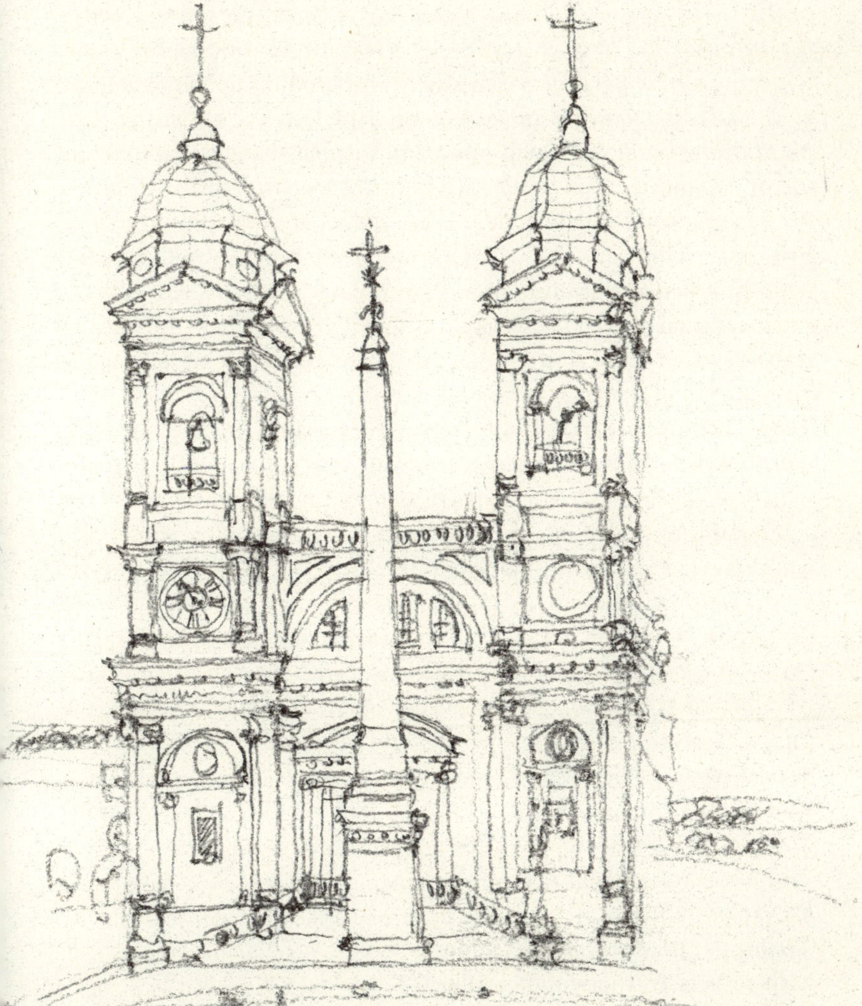

shown by the *Anamorphosis*, painted on the wall of one of the first floor corridors by father Francesco Nicéron: a monochrome fresco depicts the face of San Francesco da Paola, if viewed from one end of the room, from an oblique perspective. But if we draw closer to the painting and look at it frontally, the saint disappears, his hands become a slope, his robe a lake and his face mountains, where some of the salient moments of his life are depicted. We are at the high point of the Baroque, which wanted to surprise through the majestic use of technique. The *Astrolabio*, painted a few years earlier by father Maignan and exhibited in the next corridor, was based on the same principal. The curved face has a tangle of lines (black, red and ochre)marked with numbers and symbols: it is a meridian. A small mirror placed on the sill of one of the windows reflects the light of the sun onto the watch, which calculates the exact time in Italy, France and all the way to Mesopotamia.

These however, are not the only wall pictures in the convent. Coming out of the main structure, you go up to the old infirmary, which today houses a guest apartment. Along the East wall, where a series of rooms open up, there is a truly surprising room: the Camera del Pappagallo (Parrot Room). It was a gift by the painter Carlo-Luigi Clérisseau to father Lesueur. The artist wanted to transform the monk's cell into a true hermitage: he therefore, with pictorial tricks, created a fake stone ruin, with a makeshift wooden roof, watched over by a parrot. Above one wall, we can even see the building of an ancient temple, which would have welcomed the hermit monk. The taste for pretend is so rooted in this place, that Clérisseau even painted the blinds on the windows and the back of the door in a wood effect: a true gem.

And just think that San Francesco da Paola used to call his brothers "Minimi", to show their inferiority with respect to the Minor Order of St. Francis of Assisi. To us today they seem like giants.

41 Monastero delle Oblate a Tor de' Specchi

where frescoes speak the vernacular

For the visit
Via del Teatro di Marcello, 32
When requesting permission for a visit from the Mother Superior, you need to pay attention to the hours of prayer, as there may not be anyone to respond or receive visitors. Telephone 066795281 or write an e-mail to oblate@tordespecchi.it.

Sometimes it is surprising to think about the power of devotion a nation has towards a saint. The complex dedicated to Santa Francesca Romana, near Teatro di Marcello, is the fruit of centuries of veneration of the saint. The building was raised so that its example of morality and service could speak to different generations of Christians. It is difficult to imagine that a modest house at the foot of the Campidoglio, rented in 1436 for the dedication to helping the poor, could, in just thirty years, expand to occupy the entire block and, over the centuries, enrich itself with some amazing frescoes. As soon as we enter the convent, in the small atrium where the lid of a sarcophagus has become a watering trough, a wall is home to a painted architecture with the Madonna, St. Benedict and Santa Francesca Romana (Francesca was an oblate of the Olivetan Benedictines). This work has been attributed to Antoniazzo Romano, the greatest painter in the capital at the beginning of the 15th century, but also to Benozzo Gozzoli and to the pupils of Piero della Francesca. Even though we don't know the name of the author with certainty, the hand that worked in the convent is definitely that of a master. The same doubts crop up regarding the creator of other extraordinary frescoes, which in monochrome show the saint resisting temptation: the way in which the artist brought out the fire burning inside the devils and bursting out in the form of flames from their mouths and ears is extremely refined.

The same deep interpretation of the states of mind returns within the *Stories of the miracles of Santa Francesca Romana* in the small oratory illuminated by scenes of incredible craftsmanship. We are at the height of medieval storytelling, which however, was shown through a rudimentary perspective, respecting the lines and iconography used by Piero della Francesca. Each scene was described by a caption in vernacular, where slight dialectical inflections can be detected.

Over time the nunnery became home to more and more novices, and received donations and bequests which allowed them to carry out more ambitious projects. The enlargement of the building involved the acquisition of the Church of Santa Maria de Curte, which was consolidated and enlarged, and the construction of a great choir dedicated to SS. Annunziata, with attached sacristy planned by Giovanni Antonio de Rossi. The structure was then equipped with a refectory, completely covered with frescoes of landscapes, and a parlour worthy of a noble drawing room, where the walls host the *Stories of David* done in fresco to look like tapestries.

42 Antica Spezieria di Santa Maria della Scala
where they healed bodies… and souls

For the visit
Piazza Santa Maria della Scala, 23
To arrange a visit, which can only take place on a Saturday morning, call n. 06 5806233 (at mealtimes).
If you are on your own, you can join an existing group as the monks only open up for groups between 10 and 20 people.
Own guide.
A donation is requested.

Right above the entrance of the Spezieria dei Carmelitani Scalzi (Barefoot Carmelites' Spicery) a notice advises that the medicines for the body have no effect unless they are accompanied by a cure for the spirit: «Neither the herb nor the concoction can cure; it is your word, Lord, that cures all». Yet, the fame of this place and the popularity of these monks was not due to their sermons, but to the formidable pharmaceutical laboratory they had set up next to the Church of Santa Maria della Scala, in the heart of Trastevere. On the main altar of the church, the painting found under the stairs when work began on the site is still venerated. From the outside, on the other hand, you can go up to the first floor of the monastery, and enter some irregular rooms, where the pharmacy has remained practically intact since the 18th century. The laboratory started its activity in the 16th century, when the Carmelites cultivated medicinal herbs for their own use only. It was only in the following century that the monks made their discoveries available to the public and earned themselves the name "Pope's chemists". An extraordinary activity which lasted until 1978 and until the 1950s it also included a free walk-in clinic. This pharmaceutical activity in the Spezieria earned a somewhat legendary status. Amongst the most famous potions made by the monks the *Acqua di Melissa*, useful against hysteria, *Acqua della Samaritana*, which cured wounds and *Acqua della Scala*, a beneficial lavage for those suffering from rheumatism and neuralgia.

However, the most well known was perhaps the *Theriac*, a medicine that the Carmelites have carried on processing since the times of Andromachus the Elder, physician to Emperor Nero. It is an antidote to viper bites, made up of an incredible 57 substances including the flesh of a male viper, which was kept for years far from the sea, to remove the salinity. With the disappearance of the *viperai*, experts in capturing live vipers, the Theriac has run out too. The Spezieria still has the old ceramic vase that used to hold the *Theriac*, it is the largest of the painted ceramic containers still in existence. It is one of the decorative elements in these rooms, where even the cupboards are painted and show portraits of the great physicians of the past, from Hippocrates and Galen, to Fra Basilio, a pharmacist who in the 18th century consolidated the monastery's activities and invented a potion against the plague. He is attributed with having written the *Trattato delli Semplici*, a compendium of herbs into which all the dried specimens were inserted, along with a description of their properties. In addition to this antique text, the fascination of the Spezieria is enhanced by the original instruments used: centrifuges, presses, bottling equipment and a even a pill press, where the paste was made into pastilles ready for sale. A skilful production line that did so much good for the Roman citizens for centuries.

43 Vatican Secret Archives and Torre dei Venti

where Popes used to guard their secret files

For the visit

Viale Vaticano (Vatican Museums entrance)
The tour starts every weekday at 14:00.
To book a visit (preferably in groups) you need to call
06 69883314
or 06 69883211.
A letter sent by fax is requested to send to
06 69885574 or to the e-mail address
e-mail: asc@asv.va.
Own guide. Entrance fee.

We need to clarify it straight away that by now in these rooms there is very little left that is actually secret. The Vatican Archive was opened to scholars in 1881 by pope Leo XIII, who raised the veil on one of the most sought after resources in the world. It holds stamps, briefs and internal and diplomatic documents of one of the most active States in history, which mixes its secular and spiritual activities. We can debunk another myth: "secret" in this case does not mean hidden and out of sight, but merely "close to the Pope". The word needs to be interpreted with its original meaning, from which derives, for example "secretary", the first assistant to the prince. The documents contained in the archive have for the most part in common that they are emanations coming directly from the Pontiff. To have them close to hand, Pope Paul V decided to move them all to the Vatican buildings, assigning three rooms to them, called from that moment on "pauline", next to the Sistine Room.

The operation to transfer the documents took a good four years, from 1610 to 1614, even though the majority of the material came from the nearby Castel St. Angelo. The Pontiff had the walls decorated with scenes depicting the biggest donations carried out by the sovereigns in favour of the Holy See. A choice entirely in keeping with the contents of the archive, where many documents certifying the validity of some of the Church's most important properties are kept.

First amongst all is the donation from Constantine, upon which would be based the temporal power of the Pope, thanks to the powers and territories that the Emperor had conferred upon Sylvester. Despite the fact that in 1440 the humanist Lorenzo Valla showed that this information was unreliable, almost two centuries later, Paul V inserted the episode amongst those depicted in the Archive. The body still boast today its possession of "a copy of the donation in the form of a membrane-like pamphlet in red velvet cover and guild-silver thread finishing". It is one of the most precious documents which, together with the diplomatic correspondence conserved on the floor above, is guarded in the wooden cupboards marked with the heraldic coat of arms of the popes of the 17th century: Borghese, Pamphilj, Chigi, Pignatelli and Barberini.

A visit to these striking rooms is often associated with one to the Torre dei Venti (Tower of the Winds). It is an edifice designed by Ottaviano Mascherino between 1578 and 1580 for astronomical studies, which were aimed at reforming the Julian calendar. A new observation point was needed to identify and correct the errors of a calculation made some fifteen centuries earlier: this is where the Gregorian calendar came into being, introduced in 1582 by Pope Gregory XIII and still in use today in the majority of the countries in the world. To calculate it, the astronomers made use of the meridian devised by the cosmographer Ignazio Danti, who projected a sunbeam onto a circular plan. All around, on the walls which at one time were open to the skies, Pomarancio painted fresco scenes exalting the force of the wind and showing figures in dramatic movement: St. Paul is shipwrecked at Malta, a storm is calmed and a possessed person goes wild.

44 Biblioteca Angelica
where texts prohibited by the Church ended up

For the visit
Piazza Sant'Agostino, 8
The library is open for the consultation of its volumes.
To get to know the history of and admire some of the most ancient books, you can arrange a guided visit calling
06 6840801
or 06 68408034. All information
can be found at www.biblioangelica.it
Guide service available.
Free entrance.

Between Piazza Navona and the Pantheon there is an "Augustinian block". Nobody actually calls it that, but it would be correct to identify the block of houses framed by Piazza Sant'Agostino, via della Scrofa and via dei Portoghesi by this name. Today it is divided between the Augustinians, the Angelica Library and the State Legal Advisory Service, but at one time it belonged only to the religious order, one of the Church's most educated and active. Proof of this is the fact that the Augustine monks have never refused to accept works from controversial artists: in the Basilica there is a Madonna to whom Caravaggio gave the face of a seductive prostitute, whilst in the Library there are some texts still conserved today that in the 17th century were blacklisted.
Rather than burn them, the Augustine monks chose to store them on their shelves. Their founder was a far-sighted person: bishop

Angelo Rocca, an erudite writer and passionate collector of rare editions, in charge of the Vatican's Printing House during the reign of Pope Sextus V (1585 – 1590). It was he who entrusted his wealth of books (over 20,000 volumes) to the Augustinians, provided a revenue for the library and decided that it would be open to everyone. His example was followed by many others in the following centuries, so much so that it permitted the Angelica Library to accumulate a wealth of over 50,000 volumes, including some extremely valuable ones.

Standing out amongst these are the books acquired by Cardinal Domenico Passionei, who in the 18th century procured many banished texts, above all Jansenists, during his travels in Northern Europe as a Papal legate. Whatever has been labeled as prohibited has always attracted the most curious intellectuals. Today the Angelica is still the best place to study the debate between Reformation and Counter-Reformation, above all because it preserves the thoughts of those who had moved away from the Holy Roman Church. In the 1760s, the monks commissioned Luigi Vanvitelli to enlarge the library. The architect, who had already designed the Royal Palace of Caserta, is one of the best representatives of the transition between the Baroque style and the return to the order of Classicism. In his enormous spaces he manages to stay faithful to Classical architecture, creating some astonishing rooms. In his reading room, we are still struck by the structuring of the shelves, which has the task of designing the architecture, through its moulding and partitioning, worthy of a Renaissance palace's façade.

45 Insula sapientiae
where the heretic scientist Galileo faced his destiny

For the visit
Via del Seminario, 76
The tour of the Insula begins at the Biblioteca della Camera (the Parliament's Library). Visits take place regularly each month following a calendar that can be requested on 06 67062766. You can, however, ask for a visit on a different date, to be agreed with the government body. On other days, entrance to the Camera and Senate libraries is permitted to 250 people, over the age of 16 and with proof of identification. However, in this case it is not possible to visit the whole Insula. Guide service available. Free entrance.

The huge block behind the Church of Santa Maria della Minerva, known by the name "Dominican Insula", in antiquity it was the place of the *Saepta Julia*, a colonnaded Piazza dominated by the Temple of Isis and numerous Egyptian-style decorations. Emperor Caligula's desire to bring back into fashion in Rome the cult of the Pharaohs inspired him to build an enormous monumental area where statues, obelisks and marbles of every kind were to be found. Many are still visible in Rome, although spread out around various piazzas and palaces: from here came the black lions at the base of the stairs at the Campidoglio, as well as a part of the talking statue at the entrance to Palazzo Venezia, the famous Madama Lucrezia (originally Isis). In the area of the Minerva, two small obelisks remained, which today decorate the fountain in Piazza della Rotonda and Bernini's brainchild, the small elephant. The rest was purloined during the Middle Ages and obliterated in the 13th century by the construction of the Dominican Monastery which still occupies the entire area. Above, a private installation has been developed, made up of buildings today belonging to the Chamber and the Senate and housing their libraries. For about three years now it has been possible to walk the length of a route which crosses the two centres for study and finishes in the Casanatense Library: the so-called "Insula Sapientae".

At first sight it might appear to be of little interest, given that all it seems to offer is bookshelves and the spines of Law and History books, but it is actually fascinating. One of the reading rooms was made out of the old refectory, as is shown by the fresco still there today. Two of the decorated rooms are still known today as Sale dell'Inquisizione, and serve to remind us of how, in the 17th century, some of the most barbaric sentences in history were passed here: it was here, from a small room at that time belonging to Giustiniani, that Galileo Galilei witnessed his own condemnation. A little further on, another small room preserves the memory of St. Catherine of Siena, the nun who used to frequent to Dominican monastery to pray in a small room which, with the passage of time, has become a place of worship. The frescoes which used to decorate it, work of Antoniazzo Romano, were moved in the 17th century next to the church sacristy where they can still be seen today. St. Catherine's presence still pervades the entire complex: recent restorations led to the discovery of six lunettes dedicated to her in the Cisterna Cloisters. This colonnaded space, a true crossing point between the libraries, dates back to the 15th century, but was enlarged and reordered in the 17th century. The frescoes of the *Stories of the Saint* also date back to this period, telling of her miracles and her meeting Pope Gregory XI, whom she convinced to return to Rome from the captivity of Avignon.

46 Collegio di Santa Maria dell'Umiltà

where the novices payed to decorate the church

For the visit
Via dell'Umiltà, 30
Visits can be arranged by calling 06 684931 or sending a fax to 06 6867561. Own guide. Free entrance.

Not many historical buildings in Rome can boast feminine origins. You always read about Popes, Cardinals, Counts and Marquis, it is, however, far rarer to read of a woman who managed to have a building constructed or, as in this case, a convent. Santa Maria dell'Umiltà is entirely thanks to the devotion and clever initiative of lady Francesca Baglioni Orsini, who, at the beginning of the 17th century, acquired a block at the feet of the Quirinal, right in front of her residence, its purpose to be a convent for Dominican nuns. The lady, daughter of Caterina de' Medici, married the grandson of Pope Leo X (Medici). Her moral qualities convinced the Grand Duke of Tuscany to entrust his daughters to her. All conditions were met for her convent to have a success. In just ten short years, the nuns expanded their property and added another church which they dedicated to the Annunciation.

The entire decoration was financed by donations from the novices' families, who entered the convent, above all, throughout the course of the 18th century. Today it seems almost ironic that they chose to worship the Madonna dell'Umiltà (humility) as it was thanks to them that this complex became one of the most precious in the area. The most generous contributors were the relatives of Maria Maddalena Maccarani, so much so that she was made mother superior of the convent. The main altar in the church is attributable to them: in the chapel, where Martin Longhi was working, a painting by Perugino was hung, at that time already a precious antiquarian object (today lost). Its miraculous powers made the church very popular. The other chapels contain interesting examples of 18th century painting, just as some of the College rooms. After a brief stay by the Salesian nuns here, the building and the church were handed over to the Pontifical North American College, where American theology students stay for their studies at the Università Gregoriana and the Urbaniana.

47 San Giovanni Decollato

where the remains of those condemned to death ended up

For the visit
Via San Giovanni Decollato, 22
Visits are permitted providing they have been booked calling n. 06 6791890 (Monday, Wednesday and Friday). The complex is currently undergoing restoration work and visits are expected to start again from June 2011.
Own guide. Free entrance.

«There is always someone who will have to take care of certain things». This is how the Romans used to comment on the arduous activities of the Fraternity of San Giovanni Decollato. In Rome there used to be a brotherhood for almost every category: that of Prayer and Death, for example, dealt with the burial of the bodies of those who had no family or could not afford a dignified send-off, that of the Red Bags had the task of fishing out from the Tiber the bodies of those who had drowned. The Confraternity devoted to St. John the Baptist became famous in the Middle Ages with the name "Decollato" (beheaded), as already from the 15th century they had taken on the task of helping those condemned to death, comforting them and escorting them to the gallows. At the end of the 15th century they are given permission by Pope Innocent VIII to build a seat in Rome (they came from Florence) near the Bocca della Verità. The chest that is supposed to have collected the head of Beatrice Cenci after her execution and Giordano Bruno's hood are still kept here. The ropes used to hang the guilty every 24th June, for the feast day of St. John, were burned on a bonfire that attracted huge crowds During this rather macabre spectacle, Romans were even given hints as to what numbers to play on the Lottery. Despite these disturbing practices and the nature of the work being difficult and hard to bear, the brothers demonstrated a noteworthy culture and attention to the arts. Their church, dedicated to the Saint who died by decapitation (the same fate of the condemned they help), contains works by some of the most interesting Mannerist artists, who worked following the methods of Michelangelo and Raphael. The canvases that decorate the chapels are dedicated to the events of St. John's life, from the *Visitation* to the *Nativity* by Francesco Salviati (note the difference in style, which in the first painting is extremely sculptural, while in the second it is softer). The painter also wanted to insert a portrait of Michelangelo amongst the bearded characters of the *Visitation*, as the Master used to be a member of the Confraternity. On the main altar, the *Beheading of St. John the Baptist* is Vasari's work, while there is another *Nativity* by Jacopo Zuccchi and a second *Visitation* by Pomarancio. Walking around the church gives you the chance to understand exactly what the dominating taste in painting at that time was, dealing with the necessity to build upon the revolution unleashed by the painting of the Sistine Chapel ceiling. That work represented a true turning point, which would be echoed in the composition of the human figure, the distribution of the bodies and, above all, in the diffusion of a lively and vibrant colour scheme as had never before been tried. While Vasari managed above all to capture the monumental character of Michelangelo-style characters, Jacopino del Conte (the *Predica del Battista* is his work) recreated the contortions of Michelangelo's nudes, which were transformed into a group set up as if on a theatre stage. This particular interest in art at San Giovanni Decollato was also manifest in the organization of exhibitions for the public in the cloisters, the first ones in history (amongst the first participants was Salvator Rosa): a regular happening that contributed to the definition of the style of the age, Mannerism.

This language marked the beginning of a new way of constructing images, where the geometric precision of the 15th century gave way to drama, often represented by excessive and not so natural gestures. A device that must have also distracted and relieved the brothers during their often complex activities, such as collecting the remains of the executed in special places underground, still visible today in the cloisters: six dedicated to men and one to women.

48 Saints Luca and Martina

where the Pope gave out candles to the people

For the visit
Via della Curia, 2 (Fori Imperiali)
The Church today is still under the supervision of the Accademia di San Luca. For a visit call 06 6798850 and send the request via fax to 06 6789243.
Own guide.
Free entrance.

All the tourists who have photographed the Roman Forum have surely captured at least once the dome of the Church of Saints Luca and Martina in the background. Thousands of tourists each day pass this church on their way up to the Campidoglio from the Forum, but few stop to admire it. It is the masterpiece of Pietro di Cortona, who, as could only happen in the past, in addition to being an exceptional painter, knew how to put his mark on some of works of architecture that were amongst the most representative of the style at that time. As is the case of this temple, which contains within its structure the most intense elements of the Baroque style. Differently to Borromini, who concentrated on the smallest decorative details, the artist from Cortona essentially made use of space, which he modeled though his elegant wall plan, partitioned with strategically placed columns and pilasters. Let's take a look at the plan of this church: from the inside, it seems like a classic "Greek cross" layout, with the dome in the centre and four lateral wings. Actually, the walls seem to flow uninterruptedly, in a continuous winding course. The secret is in the depth of the four apses: whilst those of the portal and the main altar are regular, the lateral ones seem squashed. A small ploy that reduces the push towards the outside and is reinforced by the presence of the columns and the pilasters which round off the corners between the chapels. In essence, we are projected towards the centre, with our gaze on the main altar.

The architect wanted to discourage worshipers from going into the four wings which would have caused the space to lose its uniformity. These could seem like obscure considerations, but they were the fruits of study of various projects elaborated by Cortona.

He was given the chance, a very rare thing, to construct a church following only his own ideas, without any external interference. This privilege came from the fact that he turned out to be the commissioner of his own project. First of all, he convinced the Pope to permit him to begin work on the crypt of St. Martina on the spot where, a thousand years before, stood a church dedicated to her. Then, when they had found the relics of the martyred saint there, he gained the full involvement of Pope Urban VIII, who financed the building of the church and entrusted its management to the Accademia di San Luca, of which, in the meantime, Cortona had become "prince". Thus came to a full circle the project that today still conserves its features intact. Apart from the paintings on the altars (the main altar hosts a copy of the famous painting by Raphael, *St. Luca painting the Madonna*, today held in the Accademia's collection), it is the whiteness of the whole setting that greets the visitors. From the surfaces the architectural elements emerge clearly: the mouldings, the columns and all the details, illuminated from hidden sources placed above all in the central dome. The architect knew how to use light in an original way, in order to obtain the desired effect. And so it is with little surprise that the liturgical feast of light, the Candelora, has for centuries had a privileged home here in the Church of Saints Luca and Martina. Seated upon a throne of marble, Pope Gelasius, who initiated the feast, used to hand out blessed candles to the people of Rome.

49 Sistine Chapel
where you get face to face with Michelangelo

For the visit

Viale Vaticano
Private visits to the Sistine Chapel are allowed after the Vatican Museums close. They can be booked calling 06 69884947 or sending an e-mail to visitespeciali.musei@scv.va.
Guide service available. Entrance fee.

It might seem strange to find the Sistine Chapel listed among the secret places of Rome, as the over four million visitors that enter it each year have made it one of Rome's main attractions. Yet very few people know that the Vatican Museums permit private viewings of Michelangelo's work in small intimate groups, and for those who can afford it, alone as well. The memory of the experience remains with those who have been lucky enough to do it.

Walking leisurely from one side of the Chapel to the other, having all the time you need to study the detail of the *Last Judgment*, lying down on the Cosmatesque floor to admire the *Creation of Adam* or the *Great Flood*.

It could be the chance to discover some

previously unseen detail in the most famous fresco painting in the world and catch those scenes from Noah's deluge that can't be picked out when seen quickly. It seems that Michelangelo started painting the ceiling with these scenes, found near the entrance. Once he had taken down the scaffolding, which he would then re-erect in the second part of the chapel, the maestro was able to see his painting from the ground, from where all future visitors would admire it. It was only at that moment that he realized that his hard work providing the minutest details to the figures was all in vain: for the most part the details were lost as they were too far away. He therefore decided to change technique for the second part of the chapel, which in fact hosts much larger figures, created with much faster brush work. It was on this principal that the *Separation of Light from Darkness*, the *Temptation* and the adjoining *Expulsion* and the famous *Creation of Adam* were born. A little known fact which can be sampled only during a quiet visit which allows an intimate relationship with the frescoes.

50 Chapel of the Re Magi
where Borromini openly challenged Bernini

For the visit
Via di Propaganda, 1
The Congregation open the doors to their art collection three afternoons a week. It is possible to visit the chapel at the same times. For visits on other days call 06 69880162 (9-12,30) or sent email to: museomissionario@propagandafide.va. Guide service available.
Free entrance.

If ever there had been rivalry between Bernini and Borromini, the height of this was surely reached during the works at Palazzo di Propaganda Fide. It was here that an oval-plan church built by Bernini in 1644, was knocked down only three short years later to make way for a new, bigger church, designed by Borromini. All under the watchful gaze of its creator who lived directly opposite. In addition to the chapel, Borromini was also tasked with designing a new look for the building which faced Palazzo Bernini. To the sides of the entrance, the architect placed original pilasters, which widened towards the top, imitating an optical cone, while the architraves of the windows were all different, in such as way that shook up the monotonous alternating between full spaces and empty spaces. And that is not all, the façade is practically wave-like with its undulating succession of recesses and projections, as Borromini had only nodded to on the façade of the Oratorio dei Filippini.

Legend has it that in the original project, directly in front of Bernini's rooms, the windows of the Palazzo di Propaganda were decorated with donkey ears. While you need to take with a large pinch of salt the rumours circulating, still, after more than four hundred years, regarding the tense feelings between these two architects, have no doubts about Borromini's genius in working out the space in the Cappella dei Re Magi.

It is a parallel-piped construction in which the architect erased all the rough edges by rounding off the corners and turning the ceiling into a lowered vault. To exalt the verticality of the space and make it more majestic he extended the pilasters on the walls up to the ceiling, where they turn into continuous bands crossing the entire surface. In an elegant play between white and beige, these reliefs design an intertwining that imitates fluid coffer panels. It was a solution, as often happened with Borromini, never seen before: it created the illusion of a extended the pilasters on the walls up to the ceiling, with a certain sense of irony that some of the paintings destined for Bernini's chapel were relocated here, in particular, the *Adorazione dei Magi* by Giacinto Gimignani, linked with the naming of the chapel. The Re Magi (Three Kings) were chosen because they were the first protagonists of a mission proclaiming the truth of Christianity. More than their journey to Baby Jesus' presence, the church underlines the value of the message they spread throughout the world after their return to their homelands. The same objective is shared by the Congregazione di Propagande Fide, a powerful missionary institution which already in the 17th century possessed a multi-lingual press capable of publishing books in any language and with any type of characters.

51 Santa Maria del Priorato

where you can look through the most famous key hole in Rome

For the visit
Piazzale dei Cavalieri di Malta, 4
Visits can be arranged by sending a written request via fax to 06 67581270.
It is advisable to list a few dates that would be convenient.
For further information, call 06 675811 or 06 67581289.
Guide service available.
Entrance fee.

When Giovanbattista Piranesi arrived in Rome from Venice in 1740, he immediately became the centre of a heated cultural debate on architecture. His collection of engravings and views of ancient Rome which he created and sold with great success above all to foreigners, weren't only fruit of a passion for antiquity that had spread over Europe, but also the reason Piranesi found himself at the heart of a prickly question. Shortly thereafter, Winkelmann would come up with his theory of the superiority of Greek architecture over the modern one, in particular the Baroque. A judgment which offered a base for the development of the Neoclassical language. The Venetian architect responded to this view with a series of essays and collections of pictures aimed at supporting instead the value and originality of Roman architecture, which was apparently derived directly from the Etruscan one. His controversial thoughts went against the mainstream and placed his views in open controversy with the architects of the day, who no longer worked on the layering of different genres and styles, but rather slavishly reproduced the ancient order, showing little in the way of creativity. In this sense, the last of Piranesi's treatises, *Different ways of adorning fireplaces*, is perhaps his philosophical testament: a pretext for coming up with elemental compositions in absolute freedom and transversality with the same fantasy which had already characterized his famous *Prison* etchings. When, in 1764, he was finally able to create a building, thanks to the commission received from the Venetian Cardinal Giovambattista Rezzonico, Piranesi didn't miss the chance to put his theories into practice. It would be the only building he would ever get to build. It was not he who invented the famous "keyhole" – which is more Baroque in spirit – nor the garden hemmed in by tall bushes with the coffee house inside the small park, which were created before. Piranesi concentrated more on the definition and decoration of the Piazza and the church. The wall surrounding the square, marked out with evocative obelisks, served to invoke the memory of the *armilustrium*, the practice held by the Roman army every 19th October on the Aventine Hill. At the end of their summer war campaigns, before reentering the city, the soldiers used to climb the hill (which was notoriously found outside of the ancient walls) and they washed their weapons, so as not to contaminate Rome with their enemies' blood. On the standards triumphs of arms and shields stand out, with added elements taken from the naval arena, such as the rostrum on the door wall, a clear reference to the Order of the Knights of Malta. The church doesn't have a particularly scenic spot in the park. For reasons of stability, Piranesi had to place it along a slope with the façade in a position that didn't provide a full panorama. The Priory building was already in place and imposed limits on the construction of the church. The façade is a complex homage to Roman culture. The rose window opens up inside of a decoration reminiscent of strigil sarcophagi, decorated with two shelves which become snakes (an almost Borrominian quote). To the sides of the door two pilasters show different symbols: out of all of them, the most mysterious is the writing FERT, an acronym for *Fortituto eius Rhodum tenuit*, a clear tribute to the strenuous defense of Rhodes by the Knights of Jerusalem against the Muslim fleet. Inside, you are struck immediately by the absence of windows. The light enters through the rose window in the façade and from a opening behind the main altar which isn't backed up to the wall. This detail allows light to get in from behind and highlights in a completely original way the ascension of San Basilio, held up by a sphere. The saint rests on a truly singular construction, made up of a series of overlapping sarcophagi, from which a Madonna emerges accompanied by snakes and putti. The presence of upside down cornucopias (or torches?) is original and they are very reminiscent of some of the decorative elements found in the mithraea. A true pastiche, which his contemporaries did not appreciate, but today remains a proof of the fascinating and erudite project of Piranese, fruit of his intense and intelligent studies into Antiquity.

52 San Giovanni in Oleo
where the Evangelist was saved from martyrdom

For the visit
Via di Porta Latina, 17
Opening the small temple is very simple: all you have to do is go to the caretaker's of San Giovanni a Porta Latina and ask for the keys. When you finish your visit just take them back. For further information, call 06 774000032.
Own Guide.
Free entrance.

Few people know that for the most part, representations of martyred saints refer to failed suicide attempts. St. Catherine of Alexandria, who everybody recognizes by her wheel, was actually saved by an intervening angel who broke her chains, to then be decapitated: a decidedly much more banal martyrdom. The legend that St. Lorenzo was martyred on a gridiron is also false, as the Saint was decapitated without much preamble after a failed barbecue. In the case of San Giovanni Evangelista, destiny forbade him altogether to enter history as a martyr because the acts of torture carried out by the Emperor Domitian had no effect. It was decided to have him slowly cooked in boiling oil, on a low flame, near Porta Latina, close to the necropolis where he could have found himself soon buried. As Providence would have it, however, the Saint resisted the heat of the oil for so long that his executioners believed he was a sorcerer and exiled him to Patmos where he later wrote the Book of Revelations. The memory of this miraculous event stayed in Rome and as early as the 5th century A.D. it was marked by a small oratory near the old gate. When, in the mid-17th century Cardinal Francesco Paolucci was assigned the title of San Giovanni a Porta Latina, the cardinal decided to take on the task of restoring the oratory, a small but important undertaking.

He calls upon one of the most celebrated architects of the time to plan it, Francesco Borromini, who limits himself to designing a new roof (the body of the building had already been restored in the 16th century). The actual works carried out by Borromini are still a subject of debate as there are different plans of his, with historical testimony differing too. Today the dome of the small temple, easily visible from inside, is covered by a high tambour decorated with palm leaves, a lily and rose bulbs, an obvious reference to the Cardinal's coat of arms. The conical roof on the outside terminates in a spire, which rises from the top like a bunch of flowers. Once again, the architect has turned hard stone into organic and living nature: a device typical of Baroque illusion.

53 San Giovanni Calibita
where we can get to know the beggar saint

For the visit
Isola Tiberina
Visits are only possible in the afternoon. They can be arranged by calling 06 6837342.
Own guide.
Free entrance.

Kalybe in Greek means "hovel". In the 5th century A.D., in just such a hovel, set up in front of his parents house, lived Giovanni, the son of an illustrious family from Constantinople. He hadn't had a fight with his father, he hadn't been thrown out of the house, but rather, from a very young age, he had decided that he wanted to enter into a monastery and live the life of a hermit. However, over time, a new calling made him return home in disguise. First of all he camped out near the family home, then he acquired a small refuge from his parents who actually wanted to rid themselves of the unsightly beggar. It was only a few days before his death that they discovered that the beggar was in fact their long lost son. His identity was revealed to them, not by chance, by a gospel that they had given to him. Shocked by what had happened in front of their eyes without their noticing, husband and wife transformed his hut into an oratory and their house into a hospice for the poor. The boy from that moment on was known as "Calibita". The Fatenbenefratelli (Brothers Hospitallers) Hospital on the Isola Tiberina is dedicated to him, as is the church, since the Saint's relics were found whilst rebuilding work was being carried out in the 17th century. That was the moment in which the building gained its most precious decoration, a supreme work by Corrado Giaquinto, an extremely refined painter from Puglia, not all that common in Rome. In reality, none of his paintings is dedicated to the beggar saint, as in those years devotion to the Confraternity prevailed, which took over the management of the church (and of the hospital) dedicated to San Giovanni di Dio. His is the *Glory* depicted on the ceiling, where the power of Giaquinto's work shines through: the upper part celebrates the Saint, whilst in the lower part the *Fatenbenefratelli care for the lepers*. The other works of art by the artist from Molfetta are dedicated to some martyrs whose relics are kept in the church: from Marta and Habakkuk to Hippolytus and Taurinus.

The story of the *Madonna* displayed on the first altar on the right is curious: legend has it that this image was displayed outside, on the façade, right by the river. During the flood of 1577, the candle, always lit in front of the image of the Madonna, didn't go out, despite being underwater. The miraculous event triggered the immediate devotion of Rome and prompted exclamations about a miracle. The memory of this event is so strong that today on the façade a reproduction of the same Madonna is found, whilst the original is now inside, as if she needed more protection…

54 San Giuliano of the Flemings

where they worshipped the saint who killed his parents

For the visit
Via del Sudario, 40
To visit the Church you need to arrange an appointment calling 06 6872550 (Tuesday, Wednesday and Thursday morning). For further information consult www.sangiuliano.org Own guide. Free entrance.

One of the traditions linked to St. Julian has him as the unlucky protagonist of a tragic event, which left its mark on his life. On his return from a hunt, he found a couple in his bed. Thinking it was his wife and a lover, he killed them in cold blood, not realizing that he had in fact just killed his parents. Upset by what had happened, Julian decided to change his ways and chose to live as a hermit in Italy. One day, whilst ferrying some lepers across a river, in an attempt to try to save one in difficulty, he drowned. God, on seeing the profound change within him, rewarded him and over time, worship of him spread, above all in Northern Europe. The statue of the Saint over the entrance to the Roman church erected by the Flemish has a truly unusual position: resting his weight on one leg and holding his hand out in front, as if he were giving a speech. In fact, at one time, there was a hunting falcon resting on his hand, an activity that St. Julian was passionate about. It is not known who, in 1840, decided to remove it, but it may have been to save the Saint from any accusations about bearing arms. Even though it was well known that the Pope had his own private hunting reserve in the Vatican Gardens... However, the Romans evidently never felt at ease with that image which had been there for almost two hundred years. The first nucleus of worship in this place was in fact linked to a hospice for pilgrims coming from Flanders.

Since the Middle Ages the various countries of Europe have sought to ensure some form of hospitality and assistance for their citizens who made the pilgrimage to Rome. They mostly opened inns which at times also provided medical assistance. In the case of St. Julian of the Flemings, the hospital also provided the possibility for short stays, even for those who weren't ill. Inside, there is a series of paintings celebrating important figures from around Belgium: the fresco on the ceiling is by William Kent, the artist who invented the English garden.

55 San Girolamo della Carità

where you can discover an unknown Borromini

For the visit
Enter from Piazza Santa Caterina della Rota
The Church opens to the public on Saturday and Sunday at 10 a.m. for mass. Visits are by appointment.
Call 06 6879786.
Own guide.
Free entrance.

Many churches in Rome were built on the foundations of old Roman houses, where women who had converted to Christianity opened up small communities. This is the case of Santa Cecilia in Trastevere and Santa Prassede, but also San Girolamo della Carità, which rises up from the *domus* where the matriarch Paola seems to have played host to the Saint in the 4th century. In this case it was not the name of the owner of the house that entered into history, but that of the illustrious guest.

Besides his visit, the church is also known for having accommodated San Filippo Neri, who settled here after being ordained a priest and remained for thirty years. His stay, still remembered today by a small room that has been transformed into an oratory, was the basis for the church's artistic fame: it was in fact the orator Virgilio Spada who commissioned the most interesting decoration during the reconstruction works, carried out by the Arciconfraternita della Carità. Spada was the person mainly responsible for the brilliant career of Francesco Borromini, who also became involved in the building of the family chapel in San Girolamo. Even if today, scholars tend to deny its being by Borromini, some of the inventions inserted in the chapel are very similar to some of the surprising ploys conjured up by the architect from Ticino, found in other places. First of all there is the balustrade: instead of the classic small columns supporting a marble surface, the chapel is separated by a drape held up by two angels. It seems to be of damask cloth, but it is actually jasper marble, which imitates perfectly the oriental cloth. The angels' wings are carved out of wood. One of them can be turned to allow access to the chapel. Perhaps it is not by Borromini, but surely the author of this work had studied his amazing capacity to work this material.

Another small first for this Church is that it boasts the only Roman work of Filippo Juvarra. He was the architect who, more so than anyone, else contributed to the definition of the regal image of the Savoia. He was the author behind their most famous castles and palaces in Piedmont, realized through the study of Roman Baroque style, with great attention being paid to functionality. His poor luck in the Eternal City was amply repaid with a brilliant career in Europe, where he worked for both Portuguese and Spanish royalty. In San Girolamo he created one of his early works: the Antamoro Chapel, characterized by a lovely oval opening which lights up the statue of San Filippo Neri, by Pierre Le Gros, from behind.

56 Sant'Urbano alla Caffarella

where you can admire the most bloody saints

For the visit
Via Appia Pignatelli, 65
The Church is currently undergoing restoration. After Spring 2011, call 06 69886121 and agree a visit. Own guide. Free entrance.

In the heart of one of the most beautiful and uncontaminated parks in Rome, the Caffarella, hides an ancient temple, which in the 9th century A.D. was transformed into a Church, without losing the fundamental characteristics of its pagan architecture. Listed amongst the properties of the Greek politician, Erode Attico, this building holds one of the rarest cycles of frescoes from the

High Middle Ages, extraordinary testimony of the transition between Byzantine painting and the Giotto school.

In the paintings that line the internal walls, some of the most notable scenes from the life of Jesus are depicted, from the *Annunciation* to the *Visitation*, to his *entry into Jerusalem* and the *Crucifixion*. Besides vadmiring the pictorial quality of some - still almost intact - parts, it is interesting to inspect the most singular details in these images, which show how some iconography came into being only after the 12th century. In the *Annunciation*, a handmaiden appears on the threshold of the house of the Madonna: a character that would soon disappear, favouring a more intimate representation of this event. Next to the *Nativity* scene an episode unfolds, told in the Proto-Gospel of James: two Hebrew women bathing the Christ Child. A moving scene, which shows the popularity in the Middle Ages of episodes narrated in the Apocryphal Gospels. The Three Kings, protagonists of two scenes, do not wear their typical crowns, but rather Phrygian caps, the very same that protected the head of the god Mitra, a generic reference to oriental religions. The scene of the *Last Supper* doesn't seem to present any strange details, yet it is one of the oldest depictions of the meal around a table. Four nails fix the feet of Jesus to the cross, whilst later on, the feet will be overlapping and held with just one nail. Many of these scenes tend to exalt a certain cruelty and expressivity in the characters, trying to find a more realistic narration than in earlier times. At Sant'Urbano, the hieratic and apathetic figures typical of Byzantine art seemed by then outdated, but we are still a long way from the Tuscan experimentations of the 13th century. From the Apocryphal episodes, perhaps the most curious one shows Jesus descending into limbo. The frescoes dedicated to Santa Cecilia and Sant'Urbano also occupy a lot of space. The first one manages to convert her husband Valeriano and her brother-in-law Tiburzio, who are then baptized by Pope Urban I. The artist lingered with relish on the bloodiest details of the scenes of the martyrdom of the two saints, to which he added that of San Lorenzo. The blood is flowing freely and you can clearly read the sense of drama etched on the faces of the victims. It was one of the first times where the figures clearly express their emotions and visibly suffer the most heinous of cruelties. Art was slowly moving away from a purely spiritual and rigid style towards a more human and realistic one, one that knew how to speak to men in a more direct and efficient way.

57 San Nicola dei Lorenesi

where an Italian artist overwhelmed a French colleague

For the visit

Largo Febo, 17

The Church is open every day (except Saturday) from 17:30 to 19:30 for the monks' prayers.
To arrange a visit at a different time, call 06 68134563 or write an e-mail to: rome@stjean.com.
Own guide.
Free entrance.

Rome has many National churches. The most famous one is San Luigi of the French, but just as important are San Giuliano of the Belgians, San Biagio of the Armenians and San Girolamo of the Croatians. Then there are the regional churches, which see in the front line most of the regions of Italy: San Giovanni Battista dei Genovese, San Giovanni Battista dei Fiorentini or Santi Ambrogio e Carlo dei Lombardi. We should also mention amongst the latter, San Nicola dei Lorenesi, the Church founded when Lorraine, in France, was still a duchy and its inhabitants were very active in Rome. It seems that already by the 14th century a community from Lorraine was active in the Papal Curia, where they worked at the "Secretary of State", writing up bills and papal briefs. In 1508, they founded a confraternity independent of France and obtain a chapel inside the church of San Luigi. Not content yet, in 1622 they had Pope Gregory XV grant them the church of San Nicola in Agone, near Piazza Navona. Often a church entrusted to a regional community enjoys extra attention and is better looked after than the others. The Chiesa dei Lorenesi was no different, it was completely restructured and, a few years later, decorated by Corrado Giaquinto. He was the artist responsible for the entire cycle of frescoes (and two canvases) dedicated to the life of San Nicola, who is depicted as he makes water flow from stone, calm a storm and is freed by officials of the Emperor Constantine. All in all, the church represents a small Baroque jewel, with its sober and elegant architecture, which allows you to appreciate the talent of a truly extraordinary painter, who was preferred to Nicolas Lorrain, the national painter of Lorraine. Not bad for an artist coming to Rome from Molfetta, in the deep south of Puglia.

58 San Giovanni Battista dei Genovesi
where sailors were looked after

For the visit
Via Anicia, 12
To visit both the Church and the cloisters, call the Confraternity on 06 5812416. Own guide. Free entrance.

The Genoese are famous for knowing how to look after their wealth. This quality of theirs was already well known in the 15th century, when Pope Innocent VIII took the administration of the San Giovanni Battista Hospital from the Clergy and entrusted it to the fellow citizens of Meliaduce Cicala, the Genoese nobleman who had constructed it. According to the founder's plans, this structure was to be used to help sailors who arrived in bad health at the Port of Ripetta. This was in homage to those people who had worked a long time for him and had made him rich thanks to the transportation of alum from Tolfa to Civitavecchia. Over time the hospital dedicated itself only to the care of fellow Genoese and created an efficient chemist's inside, where the pharmaceuticals were prepared. In 1559, the profits from the Confraternity of the Genoese increased thanks to the privilege of being able to levy a tax of 60 baioccos (a coin used in the Papal State) from ships sailing under the Ligurian banner arriving at the port. Even today, the Confraternity, which has by now transformed itself into a foundation, welcomes mostly Genoese residents in Rome or who are up to third generation Genoese. They no longer offer healthcare, but they manage an extraordinary place. In addition to the church, which contains some significant works of art, such as a tomb and a tabernacle by Andrea Bregno, the San Giovanni complex is known above all for its exceptional cloister designed by Baccio Pontelli. He was attributed with the project of the Sistine Chapel (then built by Giovanni de' Dolci), with which he was commissioned by Pope Sextus IV, as were these cloisters, built to fulfil the testamentary wishes of Cicala. The relationship between the architect and Pope Della Rovere derived from Pontelli's youthful experiences in Urbino, where he worked with Francesco di Giorgio Martini. The equilibrium and geometric coherence he mastered at the court of the Montefeltro family can clearly be seen in his Roman architecture. San Giovanni dei Genovesi also has a dominating sense of proportion and rhythm due not only to the width of the arches, the same as in the ambulatory, but also to the octagonal form of the columns (multiple of 4, the sides of the cloisters). It is interesting to see how the corners were dealt with, as they always pose the main problems for architects: here Pontelli grafted two columns together in order to preserve the regularity of the arches. Bramante had already opted for a similar solution for the courtyard of Palazzo della Cancelleria, where the columns transform into two squared-off pilasters in the corners in order to be able to bear more weight. Today, the cloisters of the Genoese is one of the most elegant and tranquil places in Rome, decorated with a garden of roses and left to the confraternity for cultural activities.

59 Sant'Eligio degli Orefici
where Raphael left his mark

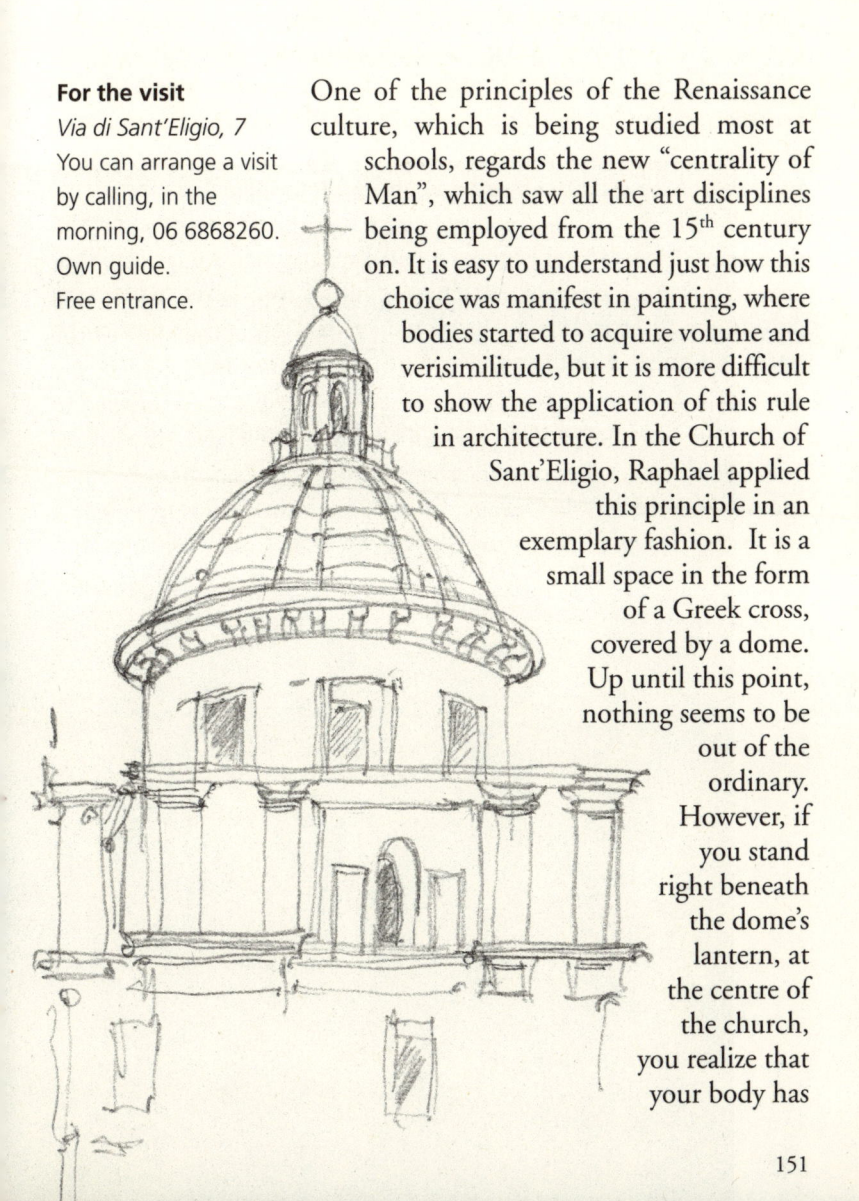

For the visit
Via di Sant'Eligio, 7
You can arrange a visit by calling, in the morning, 06 6868260.
Own guide.
Free entrance.

One of the principles of the Renaissance culture, which is being studied most at schools, regards the new "centrality of Man", which saw all the art disciplines being employed from the 15th century on. It is easy to understand just how this choice was manifest in painting, where bodies started to acquire volume and verisimilitude, but it is more difficult to show the application of this rule in architecture. In the Church of Sant'Eligio, Raphael applied this principle in an exemplary fashion. It is a small space in the form of a Greek cross, covered by a dome. Up until this point, nothing seems to be out of the ordinary. However, if you stand right beneath the dome's lantern, at the centre of the church, you realize that your body has

151

become the nucleus of the entire space and that it is possible to calculate all the dimensions of the architecture in relation to your own. You are not enshrouded by the space, as would happen in the following century at San Carlino (Borromini) or projected into space as at Sant'Andrea della Valle (Maderno and Lanfranco). You are the centre and the base from where the projection of the architecture begins. The rule of proportion and the attention to design, on the other hand, are two principles held dear also by those who commissioned the work, the Orafi and the Argentieri, who were given, in 1509 by Pope Julius II, the chance to build their own seat near via Giulia, at that time one of the most prestigious addresses in Rome.

It was here that the Pope had concentrated his project for, creating a new administrative centre for the city. Even though Pope Della Rovere's grandiose plans failed, this did nothing to deter the Orefici, who asked Raphael to design their small temple. In reality, they also, like the Pope, had to deal with floodings from the Tiber and often returned to strengthen the original building. But the fundamental characteristics never changed. Even in 1594, when the altar of the Three Kings by Federico Zuccari collapsed, the Orefici called the same painter to restore it. The façade, it seems, was only finished in 1620 on a design by Flaminio Ponzio. These illustrious collaborations are the fruit of choices made by important craftsmen, members of the Noble College: from Benvenuto Cellini to Valadier, testimony of which the University of the Orefici still holds today.

60 Santa Caterina de' Funari
where they used to make ropes

For the visit
Via dei Funari
To arrange a visit call 066785883 or write an e-mail to: info@ipabsantacaterina.it. Preferably in the morning between 9 and 12,30.
Own guide.
A donation is appreciated.

Until the Middle Ages, many place names in Rome preserved the memory of ancient monuments. In the Renaissance, new buildings and major transformations to the urban landscape often erased reminders of the past, giving the city a new identity. Let's take the case of Santa Caterina de'Funari: its name was chosen in the mid-16th century because of the many rope makers concentrated in the area. But before the Renaissance church, on the same spot, stood a monastery dedicated to Santa Maria Dominae Rosae, known also as *"castro aureo"*, from the name of the ruin of the Circus Flaminius. Over time all trace of the old Roman circus was erased and the new church forgot its place-name and contributed to changing the face of the area. Its façade, one of the most successful of the era, had to deal with a very narrow street. Its architect, Guidetto Guidetti who helped Michelangelo on the Piazza del Campidoglio, raised it onto a large base to neutralize its narrowness and enhance the vertical prospect. A ploy that transforms a typically Renaissance form (think of Santa Maria Novella in Florence) and turns it into a "Mannerist" project. The proportions created in Florence by Leon Battista Alberti, in Rome change to aid the insertion of the building into a predefined context.

The decorative instruments remain unchanged (the decorative shelves, the rose window, the niches and the doorway with tympanum), but their ratios change as everything is elongated upwards. Similar proportions are to be found inside, where the protagonist is St. Catherine of Alexandria. Worthy of a mention is the Capella Ruiz (second on the right), designed by Vignola, and the *Stories of the Saint*, to the sides of the main altar, painted by Federico Zuccari. The Saint, of Egyptian origins, was singled out as an example of morality by St. Ignatius of Loyola, who assigned the church and the adjacent monastery to the Compagnia della Vergini Miserabili Pericolanti (Company for Poor Homeless Maidens), an elegant definition for the poor derelicts who risked ending up in the middle of the street.

61 Santa Maria dei Sette Dolori

where the Lady of Our Sorrows is pierced by seven swords

For the visit
Via Garibaldi, 27
The Augustine nuns open the Church every morning at 7:15 (Sunday at 8).
To visit at another time call 06 58332969.
Own guide.
Free entrance.

There was a great deal of controversy in 2006 when maintenance works started on the Monastero dei Sette Dolori (Convent of Seven Sorrows). Public opinion feared that building a hotel here would have endangered one of the finest works of Francesco Borromini, who in 1642 was called upon by Donna Camilla Virginia Savelli to build a new convent on the slopes of the Gianicolo. Building was halted in 1655 due to a lack of funds. In those thirteen years, however, the architect from Ticino managed to leave his unmistakable signature on this building, starting with the railings. To get to the entrance courtyard, you cross through a doorway decorated with an extremely sophisticated work in wrought iron, where the bands intertwine and twist in lively volutes. The same play of curved lines can be found on the façade, where Borromini exalted elements that he had already tried out on the Oratorio dei Filippini. The building is protected by two convex lateral towers, whilst the doorway opens on a concave surface. It is not clear whether or not the exposed brick facing was due to the works running out of funds or if it was a deliberate choice on the architect's part, but it is certain that this ploy had already been used by Borromini at Santa Maria in Vallicella to highlight the monks' "vow of poverty". With him it is always difficult to understand the limits between experimentation and tradition. The vestibule in the convent, for example, harks back to the central setting of the Baths of Villa Adriana at Tivoli, from the octagonal plan to the flat ceiling, held up by four arches. Just one example of the ample evidence of Borromini's refined antiquarian culture, which, in this Church suggests some solutions already used in the Church of the Re Magi. For instance, Santa Maria dei Sette Dolori also develops in parallel to the façade of the monastery and is marked by a single continuous cornice ledge which is only interrupted to make space for an upturned funnel-shaped window, where the nuns in seclusion could watch the celebrations. The polychromed stuccoes should not fool you: they are the fruit of work done in the 19th century. Borromini refused any colours in his architecture, which had to exalt the play between light and shadow only by alternating white spaces.

62 Convent and Underground site of Santa Sabina
where they opened a precious museum

For the visit
Piazza Pietro d'Illiria, 1
Visits to the Santa Sabina complex have for a short time now been entrusted to the Circuito Aperto association.
It is possible to arrange a visit to the cloisters, the Dominican Museum, the cell of St. Dominic and the underground by calling 3279758869 or by sending a fax to 06 233201181 or an e-mail to: prenotazioni@circuitoaperto.it.
Guide service available.
Entrance fee.

The reasons to admire the Basilica di Santa Sabina are many. First and foremost is the fact that it is one of the first churches in Rome still to be perfectly conserved (thanks to the renovation work carried out by Muñoz on the building's original structure in the early 20th century). It is also worth lingering over the 24 columns holding up the arches in the nave, spoils from the Temple of Juno Regina, or over the magnificent choir made up of a collage of different ancient slabs. We are in front of one of the most refined medieval pastiches, which are day in day out right under everyone's eyes. It is more difficult though, to discover the complex's other treasures, linked both to the previous and successive history of this paleo-Christian basilica. Underground, the remains of the Servian Wall, on which the monastery rests, and the walls of some ancient houses have been found. One of these houses must surely be the house of the matron Sabina, to whom the first Christian community on the Aventine Hill is attributed. Much more interesting are the rooms of the monastery of the Dominicans, who received the church in the 13th century from Pope Honorius III. Still preserved on the first floor is the cell of St. Dominic, who founded one of the most powerful orders in history, constantly rivaling the Franciscans in architecture. Today the room is like a Baroque cell, frescoed with the *Stories of the Saint*.

In the old monks' dormitory a museum to the memories of the Dominicans has been set up, a small treasure chest of masterpieces. These range from a small inlaid column holding up a votive statue to an extraordinary painting by Antoniazzo Romano, where St. Dominic appears in an extremely realistic portrait. Between a Baroque painting and a reliquary from the 18th century, the collection in this small museum is testimony to the high level of culture which has always distinguished the Ordine dei Padri Predicatori (Order of Preachers, now commonly known as Dominicans), true intellectuals of the Holy Scriptures. They are still entrusted with the upkeep of the monastic complex: a jewel of art that continues to hold surprises, such as the byzantine fresco discovered in July 2010 under the plaster in the church's atrium: a *Madonna and child amongst saints* of a rare beauty, where no expense was spared on materials. The cloak of the Virgin is of pure lapis lazuli.

UNDERGROUND PLACES
MITHRAEA
NECROPOLES

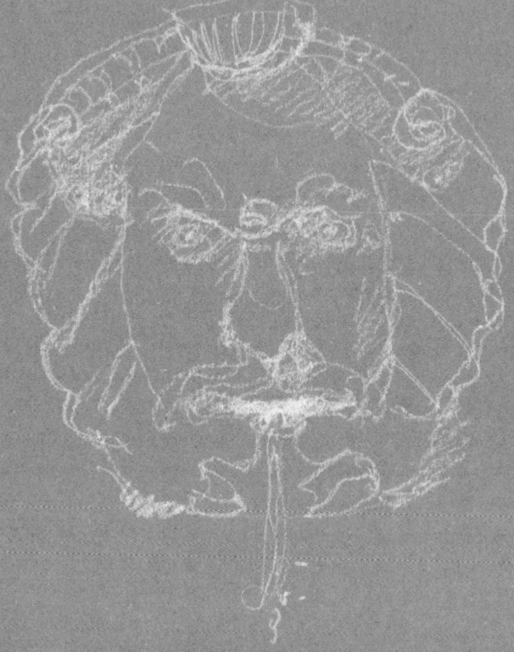

63 Underground site of Ospedale San Giovanni

where Marcus Aurelius spent his teenage years

For the visit
Via dell'Amba Aradam, 9
The management of the excavation site is entrusted to the Ufficio Patrimonio Immobiliare dell'Ospedale.
Visits can be booked calling 06 77053668 or sending a fax to 06 77053374/3495.
Own guide.
Free entrance.

In the area of Laterano the richest and most famous underground sites are probably those which run under the Basilica of San Giovanni (St. John Lateran) which contain the remains of the barracks of the *Equites Singulares* (the Emperor's Imperial Horseguards). In the 5th century, Constantine razed them to the ground because these horsemen fought alongside his rival, Massenzio. On the remains of this large structure he built Rome's first Basilica. Few people know, however, that directly next door, where today the Ospedale San Giovanni stands, a walkway has been set up to admire the underground ruins of private houses and courtyards dating back to the $1^{st} - 4^{th}$ century. They have been identified as those of the house belonging to Annio Vero, maternal grandfather to Marcus Aurelius, and the villa of Licinius Sura, legate to Emperor Tiberius. What is striking about this site, other than the beautiful black and white mosaic flooring and some parts covered with multi-coloured marbles, is the extraordinary presence of water ducts, made from crushed pottery or lead, which show that this zone was rich in aqueducts. Some of the remains indicate the presence here of fountains and gardens, serviced by an impressive drainage system. Meanwhile a tub, which must have acted as a cistern, was found full of bones in a recent dig: not archaeological remains, but perhaps dating back to the time of the plague in 1348.

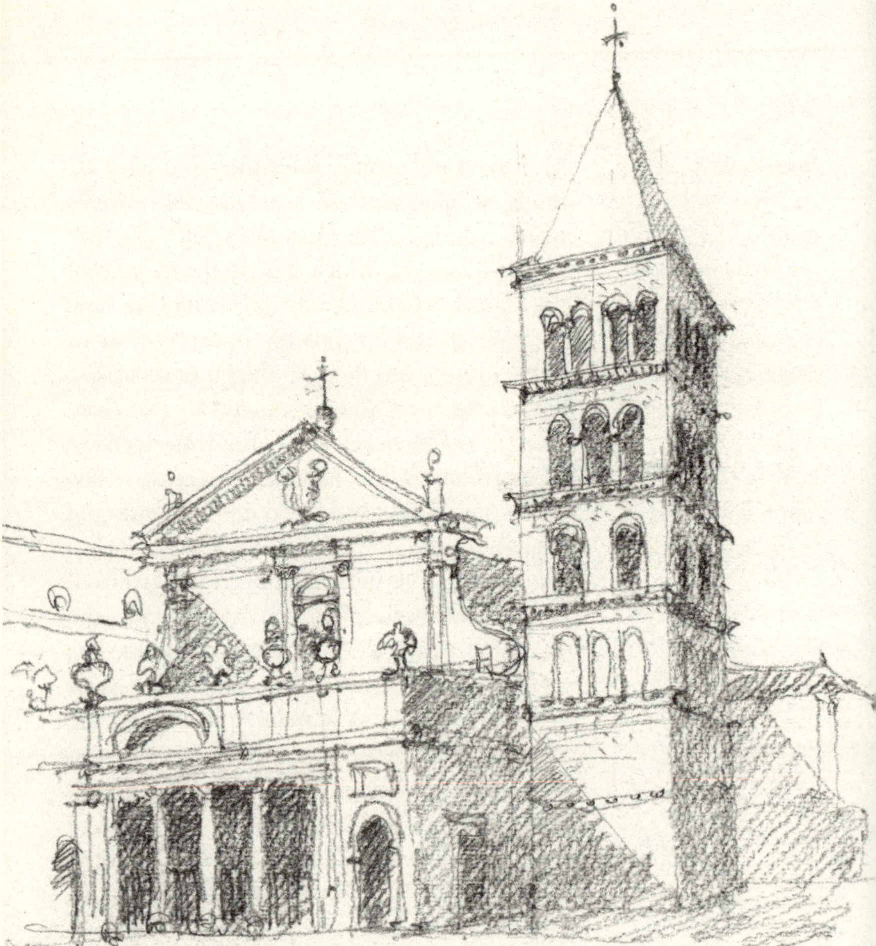

64 Gardens of Sallust
where Nero used to retire after his nightly debaucheries

For the visit
Piazza Sallustio, 21
Visits, preferably given to groups from cultural associations, can be arranged calling 06 42011597 or sending an email to info@horti-sallustiani.it.
Own guide.
Free entrance.

It was the biggest monumental park in Ancient times. And all it took for its condemnation to be sanctioned in the 19th century, was finding itself close to the new Ministry of Finance. In fact, the decay and gradual disappearance of the Gardens of Sallust began much earlier: the worst damage dates back to the invasion of Alaric's Goths in 410, the first great trauma to be suffered by Rome in the last years of the Empire. The barbarians compromised the gardens and complex irreparably, a place that for almost five hundred years had often been preferred by the Emperors to the palaces on the Palatine. The first to decide to construct a new villa here was Julius Caesar, who already had a villa on the Portuense. He donated the latter to the Roman public and built a second country house in the area of the temple of *Fortuna Publica*, his protector, on the top of a salubrious hilly area around the Quirinal. On his death, Gaius Sallustius Crispus acquired the property, to which he retired in voluntary exile after the numerous financial scandals he was involved in. Sallust's contribution to the redoing of the gardens is so significant that the Gardens keep his name, even after the emperors acquire the complex and elect it their preferred residence. After Nero's thoughtless use of the gardens, who loved to seek refuge here, far from his court, on his return from his visits to some of the Suburra's most disreputable brothels, Vespasian opened the park to the public and Hadrian had it undergo some heavy reconstruction, the signs of which can be still seen on the buildings today. Today, to visit the complex you need to descend 14 metres beneath street level, down a long and tortuous stairwell, however, in its day the structure could be reached simply by going up the hill, from where it stood above a breathtaking view of the city. Each building in the park was set out according to a precise order, to best make use of its orientation and enjoy the benefits of the sun at different times of the day and, above all, admire the numerous different views ranging from the city to the countryside. After 1500 years, the panorama has changed drastically, however, the sense of majesty and power you feel as soon as you step over the threshold remains. It has been recognized as one of the main parts of the Imperial residence, redone by Hadrian modelled on some of the buildings at his Villa in Tivoli. All around a huge circular room, covered by a ceiling worthy of the Pantheon (but "only" 12 metres in diameter), there is a complex of rooms in which you can see nymphs, tricliniums and passageways revealing the extraordinary complexity of the structure's construction. Today all the marble decorations that once adorned it have disappeared, but a large part of the main structure remains intact. Around it, there is only a containment wall, erected at the end of the 19th century when the park was leveled and dug up to prepare for Italy's post-unification construction boom. Not even the marvel of Villa Ludovisi or the extraordinary beauty of Villa Barberini, which between the 17th and 18th centuries were grafted onto the imperial structure, stopped the excavators of Giuseppe Spithoever, the main person responsible for one of the most regrettable annihilations of Ancient Rome's marvels. Recently, the complex of the Gardens of Sallust has returned to its former splendour thanks to the intervention of its new owners: Tecno Holding SpA (the finance company of the Rome Chamber of Commerce) who use it for congresses, cultural activities and permits its visit to scholars and those passionate about ancient Rome.

65 Underground site of Santa Maria Maggiore

where a misterious calendar shows ancient peasants at work

For the visit
Via Liberiana, 27
To arrive underground, you need to cross the Basilica's underground museum (open every day from 9:30 to 18:30). To fix a visit call 06 69886802. Groups can always enter. If you are alone, you can join a group that has already booked.
Own guide.
Entrance fee.

Long before the famous snowfall in August, Piazza dell'Esquilino was already swarming with people, carriages and perhaps even merchants. Today, the Basilica di Santa Maria Maggiore recalls the memory of the old Liberian church (of Pope Liberius) which was supposed to be found near the Market of Livia, (hence was identified as *iuxta Macellum Liviae*), but the structures that were found beneath constitute a serious threat to this hypothesis. To gain access to the rooms that run beneath the central nave of the church, you need to cross the rooms of the museum which hold some interesting objects: golden monstrances and precious stones, the original plans of the church and fabrics and reliquaries of a rare beauty. Along a wall a gate opens up which takes you to what at one time was called the *Macellum Liviae*, the food market dedicated by Emperor Tiberius to his mother. Today scholars tend more towards linking the interesting frescoes found at six metres depth not to the market, but to a Roman *domus* from the 2nd century A.D. Here the months of the years are depicted by showing the respective agricultural activity. The autumn months remain well indicated in the lateral, red sections. Amongst the activities shown, in addition to the harvest, you can recognize the *ludi circenses* (circus horse races) in October and the *ludi sarmatici* (games in honour of the victory over the Sarmatians) of November, an element that helps to date this fresco to after 332 A.D., the year in which Constantine was victorious over the Sarmatians and instituted the festival which was celebrated between the 25th November and the 1st December.

The long underground route offers many curiosities, such as the rich collection of antique tiles, recovered during excavations in the 19th century. Beyond proving the constant building activity in this place, they are testimony to the transition from pagan architecture to Christian, from the stamps of Cassius written in Greek to those of Theodoric from the 7th century, bearing the writing "in nomine Dei". From all the pieces on show, all in all a journey of 1400 years can be calculated, evident also in the different mural wall coverings between *opus reticolatum* (form of brickwork used in ancient Roman architecture)and *sestile*. It is one thing to study this in books, quite another to see it for yourself.

66 Mithraeum of Palazzo Barberini
where you can discover the mysteries of the god Mithras

For the visit
Via delle Quattro Fontane, 13
Visits are carried out by archeologists of the society PIERRECI CODESS. If you are on your own, visits take place every third Saturday of the month at 11:00, groups can book on other days. To book call 06 39967700.
Guide service available.
Entrance fee.

It has been calculated that between Rome and Ostia, in the 2nd century A.D., there were more than two thousand mithraea, the places of worship dedicated to the god Mithras. Today some of them have been uncovered, but for the major part of them no trace has been left. It is incredible to imagine just how such a popular religion suddenly disappeared, without leaving any mark on Western culture, crushed by the awesome persuasiveness of Christianity. Yet, while Christians were being persecuted, Mithraism was freely practiced in its "temples". The fundamental characteristic that all Mithraea share is their hypogeum-like nature. They were, since their origins, always underground buildings; underground because worship had to take place within the earth. It is said that Mithras was born from a rock, he sprang out as already a sturdy young man, with a knife in one hand a torch in the other and a Phrygian cap on his head. To celebrate in the earth therefore meant a return to the origins, to feel yourself as close to the nature of your god as possible. Part of the religion was also linked to astrology: Mithras oversaw the movement of the stars. Therefore, earth was the natural environment on which to exercise the power of Mithras. All this is explained in a fresco, which dominates the wall at the back of the Mithraeum in Palazzo Barberini. It is perhaps the most explicit and complete representation of mithraic iconography. Besides the classic slaying of the bull (tauroctony), the event at the heart of all the benefits brought by the god to mankind, there is also an arch with the signs of the zodiac, with *Chronos*-Time at the centre, and on two side panels, ten episodes from mithraic legend. The layout of the images significantly precedes Christian altar pieces, where the main scene at the centre is accompanied by tales told on the side panels. This is only one of the many similarities between Mithraism and Christianity which will be elaborated on further in the descriptions of the other Roman mithraea. What is important here, is to tell the stories of the god's acts, described in the monochrome paintings. Reading starts from the top left, with Jupiter who strikes a giant with a bolt of lightning (syncretism is obvious in this representation, where the gods of Olympus find a place too), followed by Mother Earth giving life to Oceanus, then the birth of Mithras, the miraculous drawing of water from the rock (as in the case of Moses), and the *transitus*, where the god carries the bull into the cavern.

Mithras kills the huge bull in the center of the scene by riding it (for the significance of this see the Mithraeum of Circus Maximus). On the opposite side, starting from the lower right corner, Mithras offers a piece of meat to the Sun, carrying on, the god touches the sky and the ground, proving himself to be the element of balance in the cosmos, he then joins forces with the Sun, holding a skewer on an altar, and finally mounts upon Sun's chariot, drawn by four horses. The final scene, in the upper right corner, is a depiction of the mithraic agape, a banquet thrown to celebrate the entrance of a new disciple into the community. Rather like what happens today during the sacrament of the First Communion. It may seem rather unsettling to some, but many of the rites celebrated in Christian liturgy were already present in the mithraic one, a sign that religion too is the fruit of a series of stratifications drawn from the most varied faiths.

67 Mithraeum of Circus Maximus
where Mithras killed the bull

For the visit
Piazza Bocca della Verità, 16/a
Call the booking service at the Comune di Roma on 060608.
Guide service available.
Entrance fee.

The cult of Mithras has its origins in Iran. It was brought back to Rome by Pompey's soldiers who, although returning victorious from the campaigns in Cilicia, were steeped in this new religion that had completely persuaded them. Amongst the degrees of initiation to Mithraism there was in fact a special place for *Miles* (soldier in Latin), found on the third level of the ladder that starts with the Raven and ends with the *Pater* (father). Each of these stages was related to a particular merit and required the adept to take on certain behavioural patterns during the celebrations. From the stories of the historians, who only able knew this from the tales of the participants (as it was a very secretive cult and no written documentation has ever been found), it seems that to witness a mithraic ceremony would have been very much like seeing the Brazilian rite of Candomblé, where the adepts enter into a trance and begin to utter words and make movements apparently inspired by a higher power. Helped by the *haoma*, an alcoholic drink the ingredients of which are not known, the adepts prepared themselves for the banquet of bull meat, which was consumed lying on the triclinic (cushions) always to be found in the mithraea. After having passed some secondary rooms, such as the *Apparatorium* where the priest changed, in the Mithraeum of Circus Maximus you arrive at the Triclinia. As always, at the centre of the floor there is an opening (today covered by a circular slab of marble) where the blood of the sacrificed bull was collected.

In some mithraea, as at the Baths of Caracalla, under the same opening you would find the novice, who was then "baptized" with the blood of the bull killed by the *Pater*. This act was to commemorate Mithras' greatest feat, which here is recorded with two bas-reliefs: one set in the wall to the left of the altar, another exposed above one of the triclinic. You can see clearly Mithras gripping the bull by its nose and slitting its throat. A snake makes an attempt for the wound, to stop the blood from touching the ground and fertilizing it, but a dog is there, ready to scare it away. The same end awaits the scorpion threatening the bull's genitals, another instrument of fertilization of the ground. You can see quite well how the bull's tail is already giving birth to an ear of wheat. It was the celebration of the fruits of the earth, generated from the seminal liquid from the bull, killed by Mithras. This scene clearly betrays the links between mithraic religion and rural culture and agricultural practices. To the sides of the tauroctony appear *Cautes*, a double for Mithras, who is holding a torch high, and *Cautopates*, the third twin who instead is holding the flame towards the ground (the columns that frame the scene also alternate). Above them, respectively, the *Sun* with its crown of stars and the *Moon*. Mithras determines the passage of time; he is in the middle between sunrise and sunset, the beginning and the end. Smaller, behind the bull, Mithras takes the bull into a cavern. This is how the sacrifice is consumed that gives beginning to life, watched over by a divinity who has all the characteristics of a hero, from the human face to celestial power. All in all rather similar to Jesus Christ (see the Mithraeum at Santa Prisca, p. 223).

68 Necropolis of Via Ostiense

where dead bodies were not burnt any more

For the visit
Via Ostiense, 190
Call the booking service at the Comune di Roma on 060608.
Guide service available.
Entrance fee.

The cult of the dead in Ancient Rome underwent a significant evolution with the transition from a pagan religion to Christianity. It is possible to follow this change in the different burial places conserved in this complex along via Ostiense. We are about two kilometers from Porta Ostiense (today Porta San Paolo), in an area that must have been even further from the city in the era of the Republic. Here a funeral institution created a series of columbaria. By the way they are organized, being destined for the most part for collective burials, you can tell that the columbaria were intended for families with modest means. It is not by chance that this large structure was situated on via Ostiense, not a monumental road such as via Appia, but a more commercial one. It seems, as a matter of fact, that initially it was to be used for the deceased who used to work at the port of Ostia. Simple people, content to be able to conserve the urn containing the ashes of their dear ones in a niche along with so many others. The columbarium derives its name from the shape of the typical structure used to rear pigeons, which are arranged in niches, one on top of the other. Taking an interesting chronological route, starting from the lowest level, occupied by the urns, you arrive at a zone where the columbarium begins to hold sarcophagi with arcosolia. This is an area that was redone in Imperial times, when the practice of cremation became less popular. For Christians, the body had to be left intact, as it would recover its soul at the End of Days. This saw the gradual disappearance of the urn from Roman burial practices. Burial seems also to be the method in which the Apostle Paul was interred, not by chance right here, close to the Constantine Basilica that was dedicated to him. A necropolis born to serve pagan rites over time was converted to Christian liturgy, changing also it structure.

The most interesting decorations, however, from among the decorated walls, are still the oldest ones: above a shelf that is bigger than the others are, a gazelle appears (the soul of the departed?) being attacked by two lionesses: this burial site has been attributed to a noble family, the *Gens Pontia*. Even in simple surroundings, those who were better off could afford a better tomb.

69 Jewish Catacombs of Vigna Randanini
where the "oven" burial was already practiced

For the visit
Via Appia Antica
The site is found on a private property. To visit it, call or send a fax to 06 6785989 or send an e-mail to ldgdr@tiscali.it. Own guide. Free entrance.

Catacombs were not a burial method found only in the Christian world. It seems rather, that the Christians inherited it from the Jews. This is supposed to be shown by the analyses carried out on some organic traces found in the Catacombs of Vigna Randanini: they date back to 50 B.C., when the Jewish community in Rome was already large. There have been five Jewish catacombs found in Rome. This one, near Appia Antica, is probably the oldest, and definitely the best preserved. In addition to the arcosolia and the tombs which later start to resemble the Christian model, the Jewish catacombs also hold the so called *kokhim*: a kind of oven (a narrow shaft, really) carved out perpendicularly in the wall. These were meant to favour the decomposition of the body, whose bones were removed after about a year and placed in an ossuary. On the walls of the Jewish catacombs you can obviously find drawings of the *menorah*, cedar and other symbols of the Jewish religion. However, at Vigna Rondanini you can also see a winged Victory placing a crown on a young nude male, various species of animal (peacocks, birds, geese, a ram with a caduceus), and in another room figures of the pagan Pantheon. At the centre of the ceiling, Fortune is holding a cornucopia, a classic symbol of abundance, alien to

Jewish iconography. She is accompanied by fish and duck placed between baskets of flowers.

Under the figure of Fortune, there is a seahorse and two dolphins, and on the other side, more fish. In every pendentive of the cross vault there is a Spirit of the four seasons. The walls are ornate, with flower garlands and birds. The wall at the back, now heavily damaged, showed the figure of a man between two horses. A system of decoration that has led to the supposition that these rooms already existed before and were only later occupied by the Jewish community. Or simply that the Jews in Rome were very open and welcomed positive symbols from the dominating culture into their cemeteries, wishing their loved ones well for life on the other side.

70 Monte Testaccio
where Christ was crucified at Easter

For the visit
Via Nicola Zabaglia, 24
Call the booking office at the Comune di Roma on 060608.
Guide service available.
Entrance fee.

Everybody knows the origin of this hill, built on the accumulation of crockery shards (*testis*, from which we get Testaccio) coming from the *horrea*, the oil warehouses near the port of Ripa Grande. Much less known, on the other hand, are the rites that used to be held here during the Middle Ages. After the dumping of the broken crockery had stopped, lime was used to cement the pieces together, defusing any problems regarding disease, and a bit of soil allowed plants and trees to thrive, the Roman people claimed back Testaccio. First of all at Carnival time, when from the top of the hill they used to throw pigs, bulls and boar which were driven insane as they banged their snouts and were then chased after by the *lusores*. Even more cruel was the game involving a Jew, maybe for not having paid the tribute for exemption from this torture: he was nailed into a barrel and then thrown down the slope... It took Pope Paul II (1464 – 1471) to put an end to this barbaric practice. The Carnival was in the end moved to via del Corso and Testaccio became prey to skilful merchants who, in the following centuries, opened up the famous "grottini" (little caves), the forefathers of the bars and restaurants that still exist today on the slopes of the hill. It is the mid-17th century, and Pietro Ottini, together with

Domenico Coppitelli, is the first to pour wine from the Castelli region and organize feasts, above all during the Roman October processions. While this student tradition remains and has been much developed on, another practice, very popular in the 18th century, has been forgotten. It is remembered only by the cross planted on the summit which can still be seen today. It is not the destination arrived at by a climber, rather the last station on the Via Crucis (Stations of the Cross), which Pope Benedict IV also used to organize through the streets of Rome. The Pope is famous for having transformed the Coliseum into a huge Via Crucis (in fact, still today, on the night of Good Friday, the Pope goes to the Flavian Amphitheatre). However, few remember that the Via Crucis had another itinerary, without a doubt far more scenic one. It departed from the Locanda della Gaiffa, today no longer in existence, stopped in front of the Casa dei Crescenzi, also known as Pilate's House (in via Petroselli), then in front of S. Maria in Cosmedin, finally ending in Testaccio, the Roman Golgotha.

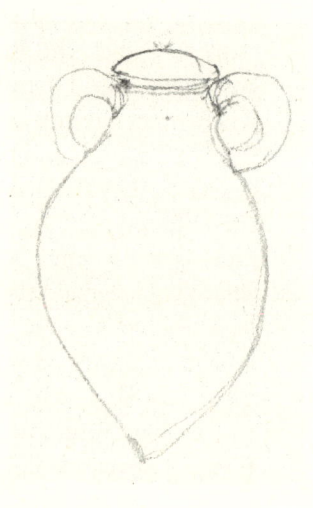

71 Lucio Peto's Mausoleum

where a private tomb was transformed into a catacomb

For the visit
Via Salaria, 125
Call the booking service of the Comune di Roma on 060608.
Service guide available.
Entrance fee.

Time has the power to profoundly change a place, above all when history removes its memory and symbolic value. This was how, in the Middle Ages, the Coliseum became a private fortress, the Portico of Octavia hosted the fish market and a private tomb became occupied by an entire community of unknowns. This is the case of the mausoleum found on via Salaria in 1887 during reconstruction works on Cavalier Bertone's vineyard. It is one of the rare Etruscan burial mounds found in Rome. The shape of the sepulchre probably corresponds to the precise choice of the owner, who wanted to give a touch of antique elegance to his tomb. The structure has been dated to the 1st century B.C., but was used up until the 4th century A.D., and not by the same family, the Lucilii, who constructed it. The initial project consisted of a tambour (a circular wall to provide support) covered in marble, where you can see inscriptions of the names of the dead, holding up a perhaps sixteen metre high tumulus. Inside, a long and narrow gallery takes you to the three rooms dedicated to burial. One of these still contains the funeral bed where the body would have lain. Only the richest of Romans could avoid cremation. It is not known exactly when, but at some point this place was desecrated. Its function did not change, also out of respect to the people already buried here, but it was chosen by an entire community to become a collective tomb.

This is why, still today, the walls of the entrance gallery are dug out with burial niches and, above all, under the funeral rooms runs another long tunnel used as a catacomb. The invasion must have been enormous, as the excavations carried out at the beginning of the 20th century also found a series of columbaria along the external tambour, which are no longer here today. Some think that the transformation was due to the family's decision, when, after converting to Christianity, they made their property available to their fellow brethren. Others, on the other hand, talk of a true and gradual expropriation due to the Lucilii family suffering a loss of prestige.

72 Hypogeum of Trebio Giusto
where an ancient building site appears

For the visit
Via Giuseppe Mantellini, 13
The entrance to the site is on private property. To visit call the Soprintendenza Archeologica di Roma on 06 477881 and ask to speak to the person responsible for the site.
Own guide. Free entrance.

Among the places listed in this book, this is perhaps the most difficult to get to, as it is found under a mechanic's garage, accessible through a trapdoor with a ladder. Visits are difficult to obtain and are suitable for the more agile and, above all, not claustrophobic visitors. The effort of getting permission and reaching the Hypogeum is repaid by the extraordinariness of the decorations. It was Trebio Giusto and his wife, Onorazia Severina, who wanted this burial chamber for their young son Asello, dead at the age of twenty-one. The images painted in the room holding his tomb provide a wealth of information about him, and also perhaps, his family. The boy appears on the arcosolium along with all the traditional student instruments: he is sitting on a stool, with a book open on his knee, with wax tablets around, a basket for the *rotula* and a *theca calamaria*. On the upper wall another figure, perhaps the father or the deceased himself, is receiving gifts above a stretched drape, whilst below it is definitely the boy, (identified by his nickname) receiving the fruits of the land offered by the peasants. We are not looking at a celebration of the deceased, but rather stories from particular events in his life, from his studies to his relationship with the fields. Far clearer, in this sense, is the scene that appears on the left: it is the only remaining image we have of an ancient building site. We realize here that in a thousand and six hundred years, things really haven't changed that much. A *generosus magister*, a master builder, leads a group of builders who are laying bricks, one on top of the other, with the help of lime and trowels, standing on ladders and scaffolding. We seem to find ourselves in a small provincial village, where family building sites still work in the same way. At that time, it was possible that they were working on a building of some importance, perhaps the building shown in the background of the fresco on the opposite wall. Here two people seem engrossed in conversation: their winter clothing is very detailed and shows how they protected themselves from the cold with cloaks and leggings. On the keystone, you can see the Good Shepherd whose presence has led to the hypothesis that this was a family that had converted to Christianity or perhaps that they sympathized with certain heretical religions, given that a single shepherd seems a very isolated symbol compared with the typical repertory of characters found in Christian burial chambers.

73 Hypogeum of the Aureli
where magic was practiced

For the visit
Via Luigi Luzzatti
Contact the Pontificia Commissione di Archeologia Sacra on 06 4465610
or write an e-mail to: pcas@arcsacra.va
Own guide. Free entrance.

It really is true that in Rome wherever you dig you will find something interesting. It is not difficult to imagine the workers' surprise when, in 1919, whilst working on the construction of a garage near piazza Vittorio, discovered a series of underground rooms, decorated, for the most part, with sublime frescoes. It is one of the best conserved sepulchres from the 3rd century A.D. A rare thing: we also know the names of some of the dead: Aurelio Onesimo, Aurelio Papiro and Aurelia Prima. Three siblings, about whom some captivating stories have been told, fruit of some dubious interpretations of the figures decorating their tomb. None of them is typical of the collections associated with a Roman funeral, but draw from the Odyssey, with Ulysses close to a female figure (Penelope, Circe?), various cities with gardens seen from a bird's eye view and Adam and Eve. The attempts to connect these images to a funeral cult have also led to the idea that there was a connection between the Aurelis and the heretic sects of the Carpocratians or the Montanists. If true, the scenes would be a metaphor for magic practices where the figures in discussion would be about to undergo initiation rituals to become doctors of magic. The basis of these theories is the Gospel of Matthew, the Apostle believed to be the first preacher of magic. However, it is more probable that these bucolic images refer to the cultural context of the time, which was about rediscovering happiness in life through contact with animals and the serenity achieved from genuinely experiencing nature. The burial chamber should therefore rather be interpreted as a *locus amoenus*, a place to take in knowledge and philosophy. Proof of this interpretation would be the presence of Jesus giving the Sermon on the Mount and many people shown holding scrolls in a stance of humble learning and discussion.

74 The Basilica and Catacombs of Generosa

where you can meet the last martyrs of the Empire

For the visit
Via delle Catacombe di Generosa
Contact the Pontificia Commissione di Archeologia Sacra on 06 4465610
or write an e-mail to: pcas@arcsacra.va.
Own guide.
Free entrance.

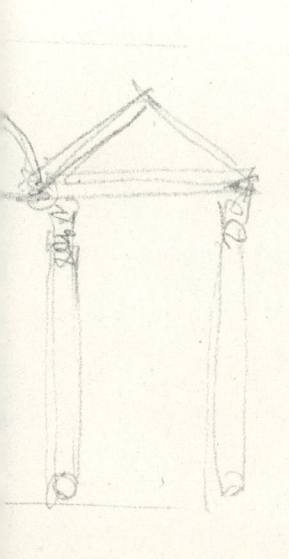

It would have been sufficient to be born ten years later, to save Simplicius and Faustinus. The two Christian brothers were among the last martyrs sacrificed by Diocletian, who in 303 A.D. had them tortured and flung into the Tiber. In 313 A.D., Constantine's Edict would have seen them released. Just as a thousand years earlier the river saved the lives of Romulus and Remus, the Tiber also allowed their sister, Beatrix, to find her brothers' lifeless corpses in the vicinity of via Portuense. It might well be a legend which makes wide use of the archetype of the founders of Rome, but the memory of her discovery would last for centuries and transform a rather peripheral zone into an important place of worship. To tell the truth, in this place at the Magliana, there was already an important sacred area, dedicated to the Arvals and to the goddess Dia. It was perhaps to deliberately erase the memory of these pagan divinities that Pope Damasus built, in 382, a basilica on the point where the tombs of the martyrs of Portuense were found. In line with the apse, a small window allowed the faithful to peek at their burial place. For centuries, access to the sepulchre took place from the basilica, also when in 682, Pope Leo II decided to transfer the relics of the saints to Santa Bibiana (today the empty sarcophagus can be seen in Santa Maria Maggiore).

The frescoes that decorate the martyrs' funeral room date back to a period just before this time. There were actually four martyrs: along with Simplicius and Faustinus, Jesus is shown giving the martyr's crown to Beatrix and Rufinius as well. Nothing at all is known about the latter, but with regards to Beatrix, a symbolic meaning has been read into her name: Beatrix would actually be *Viatrix*, she who shows the way. Obviously towards salvation, with the help of the martyred saints. More certain is the existence of the other female protagonist in the sepulchre, even if her name does give rise to some doubts: Generosa, who would have made the tomb available in order to be able later to be buried alongside the martyrs. Hers perhaps is the funeral room in which the fresco of the Good Shephard is found. Many Christians after her wanted to share in the company of the saints in heaven. In fact, under these small rooms an enormous catacomb was born, today still not completely explored.

75 Acquedotto Vergine
where the water of Ancient Rome still flows

For the visit
Viale Trinità dei Monti /Via del Nazareno, 9/a
Permission (difficult to obtain) to visit the aquaduct through the "spiral staircase" can be obtained by calling ACEA on 06 57991.
It is easier, on the other hand, to see the other site for which you need to call the Comune di Roma on 060608.
Guide service available.
Entrance fee.

Of the eleven aqueducts constructed by the Ancient Romans, the Acqua Vergine is the only one still working. A true record, if you think that it was inaugurated in 19 B.C. by Agrippa who had it built to provide water to his monumental baths near the Pantheon. Looking for new sources of water, Agrippa pushed his soldiers into the current area of Salone (near Lunghezza), where, thanks to the help of a young girl, they found the source. In memory of the young girl (or the purity of the water), the new aqueduct took the name Vergine. Today it is practically intact as the route it takes is almost completely underground, which made it more difficult for the enemies of Rome to attack. The Romans really outdid themselves with this water works: with a length of almost twenty kilometers, the water runs at a maximum slope of 30cm per kilometer. From the source to the point where the water surfaces there is a height difference of only six metres. This isn't the only record this structure holds. It is still not known exactly why, on reaching the Severian Walls, the aqueduct turns to the North, crosses Tiburtina, Nomentana and then, at the height of Salaria, enters into the city to cross Parioli (where it reaches a maximum depth of 43 metres below ground) and surface at the Barraccia Fountain in Piazza Spagna. From that point there are many fountains fed by the waters of the Acque Vergine: Trevi Fountain, the Bottino on via Lata, the Scrofa (today dry), the fountain at the Pantheon and finally the Fountain of the Four Rivers in Piazza Navona. An exceptional, monumental journey, which today is still providing water to Rome. The structure, which braver people can follow for a short tract going down from Trinità dei Monti, is a tunnel covered in lime mortar and crushed pottery, which at regular intervals opens up into a well, which reaches the surface. Often at these points the course of the aqueduct veers slightly to slow the running of the water. These are inspection wells, used to check the state of the structure and gather sediment that the water brings with it.

Today there are two ways to explore this monumental aqueduct: the more adventurous one starts from a Renaissance-era spiral staircase found near Villa Medici, whilst the easier option allows you to admire the marble arches near Trevi Fountain. They date back to restoration carried out by the Emperor Claudius, on which Pope Sextus IV intervened subsequently, as the della Rovere coat of arms shows. In both sites, you clearly feel the marvels of a work that has been working for over two thousand years and has no intention of stopping now.

76 Tempio Rotondo
where nobody knows quite what to call it

For the visit
Piazza Bocca della Verità
Visits are given by archaeologists of PIERRECI CODESS the first and third Sunday of every month. At 11 for visits are available for individuals, and at 10 and 12 visits for groups. To book, call 06 39967700. Guide service available. Entrance fee.

For most Romans it is known as "Tempio Rotondo" (Round Temple), perhaps to distinguish it from the rectangular one found right next to it. It is the more popular name for a building many others call the Temple of Vesta, as it was wrongly called by Antonio da Sangallo in the 16th century. The architect's error derives from the circular layout of the temple, where the eternal flame burned, as is remembered, but only later discovered to be in the Roman Forum. Actually, the discovery of an inscription, during restoration work carried out in the 19th century, identified the structure as the Temple of Hercules Olivarius. It was built in the 2nd century B.C. by Marco Ottavio Erennio, a successful merchant who wanted to ingratiate himself with Hercules, protector of merchants. The choice of site for the temple was by no means accidental: not only was it just a short distance from the Ara Massima of Hercules Victor which had been in existence already for four centuries, but the entire zone around the new building was occupied by the most bustling markets in Rome, the Olitorio (fruit and veg) and the Boario (meat). The refined taste that guided the development of this project is surprising. The architect commissioned was the Greek Skopas minor and the marble used was Hellenistic. The merchant spared no expense and, above all, wanted a temple that would bring Classical Greece to mind. Its simple and elegant form has meant that it has survived to this day almost intact.

Despite the danger of flooding posed by the Tiber, the structure has been in constant use and maintained over the centuries. The 15th-century frescoes inside reveal that the temple was used as a church, dedicated first to St. Stephen (Rotondo) and then to the Madonna della Luce (Madonna of the Light), due to the icon found nearby that radiated light. The final person to work on the building was Valadier, who consolidated the columns (partly original, partly from the era of Tiberius), and renovated the roofing, which perhaps originally was a dome. A form that inspired so much Renaissance and Baroque architecture.

77 Pyramid of Caio Cestio

where you can admire the most exotic tomb in Rome

For the visit
Piazza Ostiense /Via del Campo Boario
Visits are conducted by the archaeologists of PIERRECI CODESS the second and fourth Saturday of each month. At 11 for singles, at 10 and 12 for groups.
To book call 06 39967700. Guide service available. Entrance fee.

Everybody knows it from outside, but few people know what it contains. Yet in the last few years, a great deal has been done to attract visitors to the Pyramid, which at one time would draw huge crowds to its impromptu openings. Today visits are regular and offer the chance to enter into the bowels of one of the most mysterious monuments in Rome, still with us today due to an entirely fortuitous reason. In the Middle Ages, there were four pyramids in Rome: two at the beginning of via Lata, more or less where the "twin churches" stand today, one near the present-day via della Conciliazione (but knocked down long before Mussolini's interventions) and this one, which still looks over the skies of Testaccio. The last two became for the Romans the mythical resting places of Romulus and Remus, until widespread superstition transformed them into esoteric and diabolic places, a sign of the presence of evil in the city. And yet, the pyramid at Ostiense is merely the fruit of one wealthy Roman's mythomania, that of Caio Cestio, remembered on an inscription as Triumvir of the Epulones. He was one of the people in charge of organizing the Emperor's sacrificial banquets for the gods. Perhaps it was the same Caio Cestio who found himself, in the 1st century B.C., in Asia Minor and returned to Rome with a passion for oriental cults. What is certain is that he constructed his tomb (in only 330 days) before Augustus emanated the *lex sumptuaria*, forbidding luxury burials. Lucky for him, as he was able to build a sepulchre, which would have him remembered for all time. He placed his sarcophagus inside, and maybe also his treasure, as every self-respecting pharaoh did. The possibility of finding treasure caused someone at a certain point to desecrate the pyramid by tunneling into the burial chamber. The signs from his breaking in are still visible. He first started digging on the wall opposite the entrance tunnel (at the time filled with earth and invisible from the outside), but he found nothing. Not content, he stuck two beams into the walls at the height of the curve in the vault, where he placed a platform and made holes in the ceiling, destroying the fresco of the deceased painted there. In all probability, he found nothing there either and came out empty-handed. Work at the time of Pope Alexander VII had reopened the entrance gallery and permitted scholars to document the decorations, which today are rather worse for wear. Winged Victories in the corners of the vault and candelabras bring out the paintings on the walls of vendors selling: a refined example in the Third Pompeian style. Proof that the work was spared no expense. The longevity of the monument has been due to its position: as luck would have it, the Pyramid found itself in the path of the Aurelian Wall, built at the end of the 3rd century. From a private burial place, it was transformed into a defensive structure, kept up until the end of the 19th century. At one time, the soldiers could get around it thanks to a wooden walkway running around it. Today, there is no longer any trace of this contraption, but along the walls which face onto the garden you can still see the rings from which Petrarch saw festoons hanging on the occasion of a public festival in the 14th century.

78 Jewish Catacombs of Villa Torlonia
where no human figures appear

For the visit
Parco di Villa Torlonia
Contact the Soprintendenza Archeologica di Roma on 06 477881 and ask to speak to the person responsible for the site.
Own guide.
Free entrance.

What definitively refuted the false idea that the catacombs were a clandestine meeting place for Christians, was the discovery of the Jewish catacombs in Rome. Even the Jews, who in the city had a large and, above all, not troublesome presence for the Emperor, had chosen catacombs as the burial method for their members. Clearly, they weren't given permission to build large monuments, which would have caused no small embarrassment to the official religion. Better underground, where it was possible to carry out their rites in tranquility. Testimony to this are the Jewish catacombs in Rome, amongst which the ones at Villa Torlonia are perhaps the easiest to decipher. The entrance on the surface leads to a room where rites regarding the preparation of the deceased's body were carried out, and the final salute was given. After this, came the *kokhim*, a kind of modern oven that helped the corpse to decompose, leaving behind just the bones, which, after about a year, were moved into the loculi. Some of these are marked specially by columns carved out of the tuff, which show the door and the four corners of the funerary cell.

Here too, as in all catacombs, there are many found belonging to children. However, what sets these burial places apart is the total absence of human figures in the decoration.

As representation of *Jehovah* was not allowed, the Jews often depicted only the *menorah*, surrounded by dolphins, pomegranates and legal scrolls.

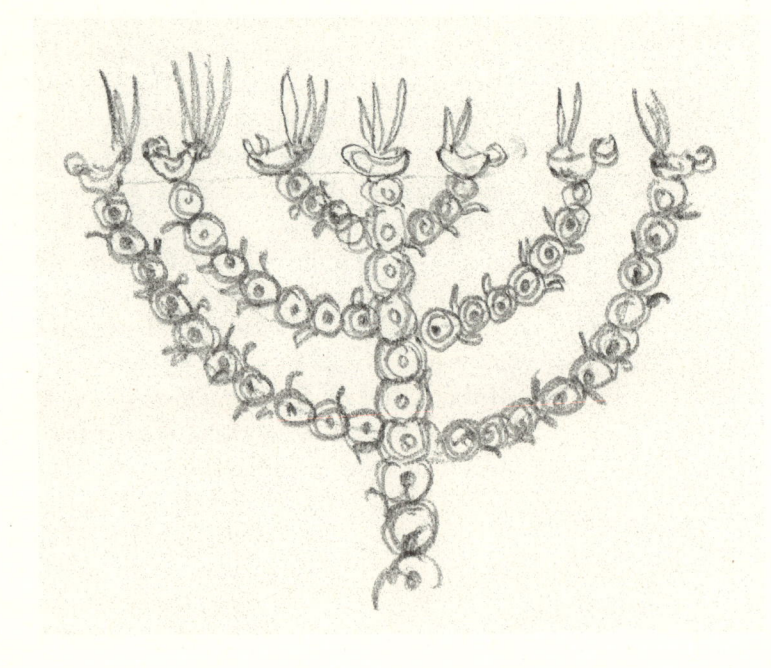

79 Tombs of Via Latina
where you lose track of time

For the visit
Via dell'Arco di Travertino, 151
Visits are conducted by archaeologists of PIERRECI CODESS.
For individuals, visits take place on the second and fourth Saturday of each month at 11.
For groups, at other times. To book, call 06 39967700.
Guide service available.
Entrance fee.

In addition to the lovely funeral rooms, the park of the Tombe (tombs) di Via Latina offers a unique experience, only a short distance from the Historical Centre. Here, it is like taking a stroll through a zone where time stands still and the few buildings standing here have been saved from the concrete invasion. Along an ancient road, you can see the tombs of important figures, some decorated with stuccoes of a rare beauty, which have miraculously survived over the centuries, despite occupation by shepherds and farmers. Little has changed since when, in the 19th century, Fortunati first discovered them on one of his many digs looking for precious archeological finds to sell to the Vatican or put on the antiques market. From amongst them all, the most elegant is perhaps the Tomb of the Valerii. Do not let the building's elegance fool you; it was redone completely in the 19th century. The stucco work on the ceiling (2nd century A.D.) is original: satyrs, maenads and nereids who accompany the funerary rites. The elegance of this work is not only due to its purity but also to the incredibly light movements of the figures. The spirals that whirl around on the entire surface cause certain Renaissance works to pale by comparison in their elegance, while the figures, even though they appear in emptiness within the medallions, have an almost three-dimensional volume and presence. They are animated and playing as if caught in live action. The same impression, but enriched with an almost intact colouring, is given by the frescoes of the Tomb of the Pancrazi. In this case, the repertoire is clearly that of the Olympian divinities, who surround the representation of Jupiter at the centre of the ceiling (perhaps a portrait of the deceased). Admetus is accompanied by Apollo and Diana, Paris is in the throes of assigning the famous apple and Hercules is being welcomed among the gods.

The work is speckled with dancing figures, cherubs playing, figures of the demi-gods and bucolic landscapes alternating on the stuccoes and frescoes. A true jewel restored from antiquity, which raises the thought of just how many more tombs just outside Rome house even richer and more precious decorations.

80 Basilica and Catacombs of San Valentino

where the protector of lovers is buried

For the visit
Via di San Valentino
The site is currently under restoration due to collapses that took place over a year ago on the Parioli hill.
To see if it is possible to arrange a visit, contact the Pontificia Commissione di Archeologia Sacra on 06 4465610
or write an e-mail to: pcas@arcsacra.va.
Own guide. Free entrance.

We don't know with any certainty whether the St. Valentine buried at the foot of Parioli is really the protector of lovers. Some documents dating back to the 4th century A.D. tell us that he was martyred on the 14th February in Rome. In 496, Pope Gelasius I instituted the festival dedicated to the saint on the day of the *Lupercalia*, rites that were already dedicated to fertility. In the following century, Pope Julius I perpetuated his memory with the construction of a Basilica. The tomb of the Saint was set apart from the necropolis where he had been found and made more visible in order to facilitate access to it by pilgrims.

Today, what remains of this structure are two apses, whilst a short distance away, some of the rooms of the catacomb, linked to the memory of the martyred Saint, are also open to the public. It used to be a very common practice to try and find a burial place close to someone who could put in a good word for you to St. Peter. Very few traces remain of the paintings on the walls (only fragments of a *Madonna and child*), but Antonio Bosio, in the 16th century, had the opportunity to see them intact and describe them. At that time, it was still possible to see a *Crucifixion*, with the Madonna and some saints holding books and crowns of the martyr.

81 Hypogeum of Via Dino Compagni

where you can admire an ancient lesson in medicine

For the visit
Via Latina, 258
Contact the Soprintendenza Archeologica di Roma on 06 477881 and ask to speak to the person responsible for the site.
Own guide. Free entrance.

It cannot have been a nice surprise for the workers in 1955 who were putting down the foundations for a new building on via Latina. Without warning, the ground gave way and revealed an underground room completely covered in frescoes. Risk of closure for the works was not far off. Rumours spread and some tried to profit from it by breaking off some of the pictures, but the competent authorities were only alerted at the close of the works, by which time the archeological site could only be set up precariously. The fate of this hypogeum would have been different had the news of this discovery been relayed earlier. We find ourselves in front of an extraordinary monument, known as "the Art Gallery of the 4th century" for the quality and quantity of its pictures. It is an extensive funereal complex built in the 4th century A.D., at a time when the Christian and pagan religions lived together in harmony, thanks to Constantine's edict in 313 A.D. The great cohesion between the rooms in this hypogeum and the fact that it was used for only fifty years led archaeologists to believe that it can be attributed to a single family. However, not all of the members of the family seem to have converted to Christianity: the decorations show both classical myths and scenes from the Bible. In the first "chapel", shown on an arcosolium is a female figure lying on a lawn, with a serpent around her left arm: immediately it was thought to be Cleopatra, but today thought tends towards identifying her as *Tellus*, Mother Earth.

The cubicle next door is, on the other hand, without a doubt dedicated to Hercules, hero of the story of Admetus and Alcestis (the hero brought her back to life from Hades which she entered for a sacrifice of love): the frescoes on the four walls are dedicated to his labours. In the Christian chapels, the themes are all connected to the passage between life and death: the Jews crossing the Red Sea which opened up to Moses, Lazarus rising from the dead thanks to Jesus, Abraham meeting God at Mamre. The last room possibly housed the body of the young girl with the big dark eyes and hair tied back on her neck, who is shown in the decorations. Her family must have been the richest as this is the only cubicle with an abundance of marble. A mystery accompanies the uncertain interpretation of the so-called "lesson in medicine": an arch shows a group of men in togas gathered around the laid out body of a dead infant. A bearded man (philosopher?) touches the stomach with a rod. Are we witnessing a lesson on the soul?

82 Cloaca Maxima
where you can walk in the oldest sewer in Rome

For the visit
Access from the Trajan Forum
Access is only given if previously requested from the Sovraintendenza Comunale.
Call 06 67103238 and ask for the contact numbers for the person responsible for the Trajan Forum to agree a visit. Own guide.
Free entrance.

It may seem strange to be invited to explore the place where all the excrement and rubbish from ancient times ended up (there is even some from today), but the Cloaca Maxima is one of the most incredible works from Ancient Rome. It still works after an incredible twenty-seven centuries. The water still runs in its conduits and flows into the Tiber near Ponte Rotto. It was built by King Tarquinius Priscius in the 6th century B.C., to help the lives of the various communities that had descended from the "seven hills" to colonize, amongst others, the Tiber valley. It seems that the King was helped by Etruscan know-how, as they were already experts in works of this kind. At first, it was an open-air channel which flowed into the Tiber, a confluence point for the waters – the natural stream of which came down from the hills – and an efficient instrument for draining the Forum and the Velabrum, little more than marshland in those times. Small streams lost from memory: the *Amnis Petronia* between the Pincian and the Quirinal Hills, the *Spinon* between the Quirinal and the Esquiline Hills and the *Nodinus* between the Esquiline, Caelian and Aventine Hills. The Cloaca even back then used to cross the heart of the city. The need for more building space forced the Romans to cover the channel and reinforce its structure with round arches, which are still visible underground. The material used the most for the support structure was *gabinus* stone (dark tuff), which, due to its fire resistant properties, would have guaranteed greater strength for the structure.

The Romans were far-sighted. You can explore the conduit from various points. The easiest to access passes under Nerva's Forum, near Tor de'Conti, and shows bits with different coverings, from tuff overburden, from travertine marble (precious, yet used in a sewer) to crushed pottery clay. Although the air you breathe inside the Cloaca is still not pleasant, walking along these canals (an experience not to everybody's taste) allows you to get a clear idea of the concrete and proactive intelligence of the Ancient Romans. Sophisticated even in the most functional and least celebrated works of their greatness, yet still admired today as one of their masterpieces.

83 Syriac Sanctuary
where they found the mysterious God wrapped in the coils of a snake

For the visit
Via Dandolo, 47
The site has recently manifested some problems with its security due to problems in the apse, but if you ask the person in charge it is still possible to obtain permission to visit.
Call 06 68485162 or send a fax to
06 6897091.
Own guide.
Free entrance.

In Rome, as it is known, there has always been great religious tolerance. Before the Christians posed a threat to the supremacy of the Emperor, all cults were allowed. Some convened in places shared by different religions. It seems that this is the case with the so-called Syriac Sanctuary, which is found near one of the secondary entrances to Villa Sciarra. Slaves, freemen and foreigners from every corner of the Mediterranean gathered here to worship their gods. The different idols found in this place show that there was space for Egyptians, Libyans, Syrians and the faithful of all the oriental religions that had found a home in Rome. A Jupiter on a throne must have lived in one of the niches, while a little further on resided Osiris, shown here as a pharaoh with golden hands and face. However, of them all, the most unsettling and mysterious image found in this place is a statue not more than 50 cm high. It is of a young man wrapped up in a shroud, as if he were a mummy. A serpent is coiled all around his body with its head resting on top of the human figure's. It is still not known to which religious sect this object refers. In addition to its singular iconography, the mystery is further complicated by the place in which it was discovered, a small triangular recess.

As is known, the triangle is an archetype common to many religions, always known to have magical connotations. It is probable that the statue represents a character that has something to do with death and regeneration, perhaps Adonis, maybe Simios, his presence linked to the passing of the seasons and the salvation of the soul. Many agree that this place was used for initiation rites. The central courtyard, instead, was used for gatherings, but around which divinity, is as yet unclear…

84 Necropolis of Villa Pamphilj
where over five hundred people found a worthy resting place

For the visit
Via Aurelia Antica, 111
Contact the person at the Soprintendenza Archeologica responsible for the site on 06 684855116 or send a fax to 06 6897091 (often they are out making inspections, so be patient).
Own guide.
Free entrance.

The level of civilization of a population can be judged by the way they treat their dead. The more complex and populated the afterworld is, the richer a people's culture is. In the case of the Ancient Romans, the different types of sepulchres show a profound faith in their belief of life after death. In Rome, there weren't only monumental mausoleums, those of the Emperors and the nobility on Appia Antica, but along all the main streets there were necropoles of varying styles. Every social class had the right to a dignified burial. The most frequently seen tombs are the columbaria, scattered around the city: they can be found along the via Ostiense, Appia, Flaminia and Aurelia. There is also a necropolis in the park of Villa Pamphilj, close to the Casino dell'Algardi, which being a government building, makes visits to the site a bit more difficult (due to security reasons). In the sepulchre, in 1984, over five hundred niches were found where the urns of as many people resided, each one remembered with a nameplate. Often these collective sepulchres were built by a wealthy family, who sold places to people who needed them and allowed access to family members who would periodically come to carry out the funeral rites. The regular visits to these columbaria justified their decorations which, at times, were excellent.

At Villa Pamphilj, the most important frescoes have been taken down and now hang in the Museum of Palazzo Massimo. Lesser fragments however, remain: animals and pygmies fighting with cranes and riding rams. A surround of scenes, that must have created a light and serene context next to the figures of the divinities close to the dead.

85 The Columbarium of Pomponio Hylas
where two griffins keep the evil eye at bay

For the visit
Via di Porta Latina, all'interno del Parco degli Scipioni
Contact the booking service of the Comune di Roma by calling 060608.
Guide service available.
Entrance fee.

In ancient times, whoever could not afford a private burial chamber registered with a funeral association, which, against the payment of a modest sum, assured that the ashes of the dead would be welcomed in a columbarium. Possibly the most interesting one, that we still have today, is the one that has been identified as that of Pomponio Hylas. It was hidden underground in the Parco degli Scipioni, under a small cabin that looked more like a tool shed. Instead, on going down the narrow access stairs, you immediately see a beautiful mosaic inscription, remembering the name of the developer of this collective sepulchre and his wife, Pomponia Vitalinis (who at that time was still alive, as indicated by a letter "v" above her name). Under the inscription are two griffins either side of a cithara (lyre-like instrument) which have an apotropaic function, to ward off the evil eye. Religion and superstition in Ancient Rome were the same thing. The columbarium probably already existed in Hylas's day, to whom a restoration and management of the structure have been attributed. This suspicion derives from the fact that in the main niche reside the ashes of two other people: Granius Nestor and Vinileia Pedone, who are shown in portraits with a scroll in hand next to a basket, typical elements from the Dionysian ritual. Beneath

luxuriant vegetation, which transforms the sepulchre into a welcoming garden, there are many niches, some richer, some simpler.
It depended on the money the deceased had available. Here, they must have had a great deal to be able to build a miniature temple decorated with scenes of Chiron giving life lessons to Achilles, in relief on a blue background.

86 Mausoleum of Monte del Grano
where a double homicide is commemorated

For the visit
Piazza dei Tribuni
Contact the booking service of the Comune di Roma by calling 060608.
Guide service available.
Entrance fee.

Even if the debate is still open, the mausoleum that rises in the heart of the Quadraro must have had something to do with one of the imperial families of Rome. If for no other reason than it being the third in order of size after Castel Sant'Angelo and the Mausoleum of Augustus. It wasn't the easiest of things competing with the tombs of the Emperors if one didn't belong to a similar class. Many people still argue over which Emperor it was built for, but there is no doubt regarding its grandeur. It lies under a barrow which today goes almost unnoticed, but, in the 18th century, Piranesi had already crossed its 21 metre long corridor, which leads to a room 10 metres in diameter. The vault, done in Roman brick, is the work of very expert hands, used to constructing majestic monuments. The floor was originally in marble, as must have been the stucco decorations on the false vaulted ceiling, which was lower than the current one. The name of this place is linked to a legend: its shape is reminiscent of an enormous overturned bushel of wheat. It is said that a bolt of lightning transformed it into earth as a punishment since it was gathered on Sunday, the day sacred to the gods. One of the clues that points strongly to the attribution of this sepulchre was a celebrated sarcophagus found in the 16th century. It must have held the bodies of two people, portrayed on the cover, lain out in the Etruscan manner.

It is assumed that they are Alessandro Severo and his mother, Giulia Mamea, assassinated in Magonza in 235 A.D. The bulk of the object required a well to be opened (still in existence) to transport the sarcophagus to the surface to then be donated to the Pope. Today it is on exhibit in the Capitoline Museums.

87 Mausoleum of Sant'Elena
where blocks hold up the dome

For the visit
Via Casilina, 602
The site is currently under restoration. It is due predicted to be reopened in spring 2011.
For information, contact the person responsible for the site at the Soprintendenza Archeologica di Roma on 06 6977671.

Torpignattara today is a place name linked to one of the suburbs on the farthest outskirts of Rome. It almost sounds like a swear word, but it refers instead to a particular characteristic of the noble Mausoleum of Elena, Constantine's mother. In the 4th century A.D., to lighten the weight of the dome, empty amphorae were inserted, known as *pignatte*. Torpignattara, therefore, indicates a valuable and ancient architecture. It seems that the building was actually destined for the Emperor himself, who had occupied the area that had previously been dedicated to the necropolis of the Imperial Horseguard – the same horseguards that had defended his rival, Massenzio. After having razed their barracks to the ground at Lateran, in order to build the Basilica di San Giovanni, he also eradicated their sepulchres on via Casilina. When his mother passed away, the Emperor decided to give the Mausoleum to Elena. This is where the famous red porphyry sarcophagus comes from that greets visitors in the Vatican Museums.

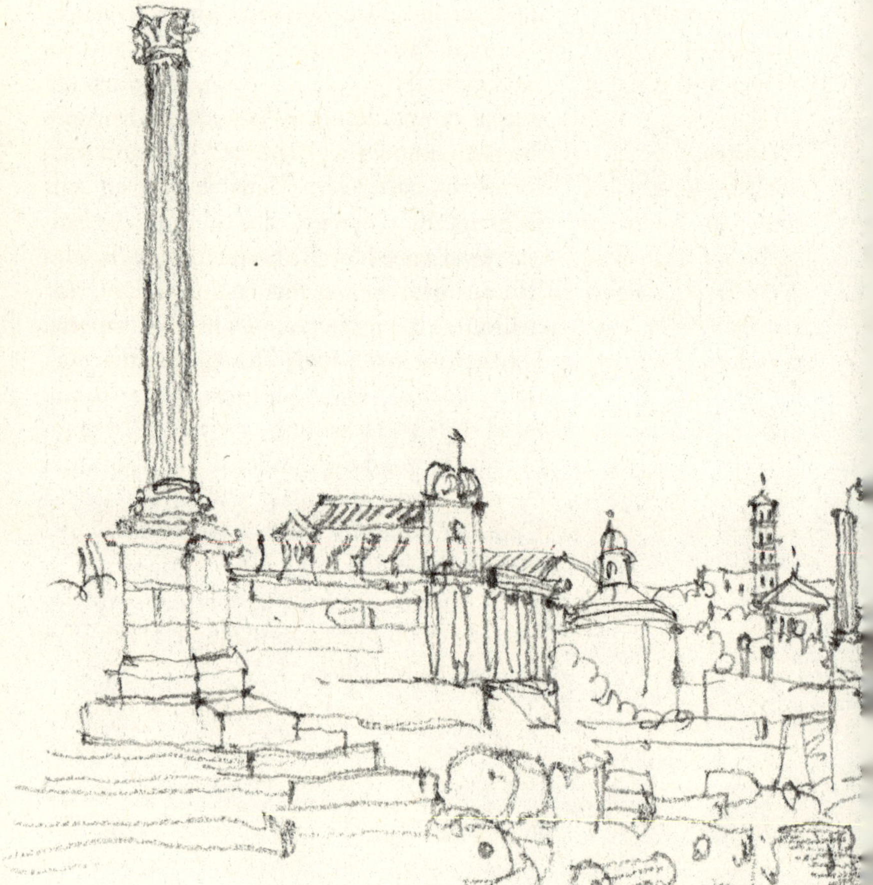

88 Imperial Forum
where you can go through an unknown underground tunnel

For the visit
Enter from Trajan's Column
The site can only be accessed with prior consent from the Sovraintendenza Comunale.
Call 06 67103238 and ask for the numbers of the people responsible for Trajan's Forum to agree a visit.
Own guide.
Free entrance.

The fact that they can be admired from via dei Fori Imperiali has for years given the people in charge at the Ministry of Cultural Heritage the excuse to delay opening Trajan's, Augustus', Nerva's and Caesar's Fora up to the public. Effectively, managing them would require dozens of custodians. Yet, admiring the remains of the *Basilica Ulpia* and the *Temple of Mars Ultor* from the inside is a different thing entirely, above all in the last few years, since it was discovered that *Trajan's Column* did not represent the end of the Forum, but rather the beginning, in the courtyard onto which the Emperor's two libraries faced. These buildings were so tall that it was possible to see up close, from their top floors, the events sculpted on the Column surrounding Trajan's victory over the Dacians.

Today, this is still the departure point for exploring this area, which, along with the Roman Forum represents the largest archaeological park in the world in the heart of a modern city. Although it was, and still is, a much-criticized decision by experts, Mussolini's idea to re-erect the columns of the Basilica Ulpia created an extraordinary effect. Walking around these pavonazzo-blue marble columns evokes an intense feeling of the dynamic activity that used to take place here. Unfortunately, the close proximity to the present-day street doesn't allow us to truly appreciate its originality: it was the only basilica with two apses. The entrance, as is still the case today, was from the lateral walls.

Having crossed the Basilica, you arrive in the Forum itself. An enormous piazza, where the most recent excavations have restored the shapes of the marble slabs that used to cover the floor. A large part of this area still houses the walls from medieval constructions: an oven, workshops and the rooms of an ancient monastery, which was also used as a hospital. From inside, you can see the enormous antique marble inserts, put together randomly to pull up the walls quickly. Here you can see parts of columns and huge fragments of decorated ceilings. One room is entirely taken up by two yellow-marble column pieces: they belonged to the Forum's portico which collapsed, who knows when, and were never moved. It is in this zone that a slab shows us where the large equestrian statue of Trajan stood, in the heart of the Forum. It was the statue's position, directly facing the Column that led archaeologists to re-orientate the entire complex. Another recent discovery, at the end of the 1990s, was the so-called "area sacra". After having admired the human accomplishments of Trajan, visitors were able to participate in worship of the Emperor, who here became *Divus* (divine, as did all the sovereigns after their death). There are extraordinary fragments of green, red and white marble that give an indication as to just how special this area was. Passing under an arch that holds up Via Alessandrina, you enter into Augustus' Forum. Even in Ancient Times, the passing from one Forum to another was continuous and it is a privilege to be able to relive the same route today. This area is dominated by the great wall that Augustus had erected, to protect his forum from the frequent fires that broke out in the Suburra district. He chose to use *gabinus* stone for its fireproof properties.

You can see today the marks left on this imposing wall by the sloping roof of the Temple of Mars Ultor, erected as an ideal retaliation to Caesar's death, thus gaining favour with the people. You can still go up the stairway that leads to the Temple's entrance. Walking a little further on, you enter Nerva's Forum, long and narrow, which inherited the old structure of Domitian's portico. The only element that remained in place is a fragment of the frieze that ran around the Forum, where you can still see today some depictions of Roman provinces (homage to the Empire and an act of populism) between episodes recounting the legend of Arachne, the woman transformed into a spider for having challenged Athena.

In order to be able to cover the whole area of the Forum, you now have to cross the so-called "chiavicone". A sewer conduit, possibly from the 17th century, which passes under the traffic-laden via dei Fori Imperiali. Narrow and dark, it reminds you how the Imperial Fora are still divided into two areas by an artery, which doesn't permit you to enjoy its unity. Of the monuments dedicated to Nerva, few remain on the other side and your attention is immediately drawn to the recent excavations of the proto-historic necropolis. This is where the first inhabitants of the marshes between the Palatine and Campidoglio Hills were buried. Before Romulus and Remus, even before Rome, this area was already inhabited. On this earth, Caesar would build the first of the Imperial Fora and create the model that would be followed by all his successors: a large piazza, a temple and a zone destined for markets and commerce. Even though the dictator was never a true Emperor, both with regards to politics and architecture he inaugurated all the choices that from Augustus on would determine the politics of the governors of Rome. On one side, the weight of his military successes, on the other, the conception of monumental architecture in which he could show his glory, perhaps with the help of the Gods. Venus Genetrix waits at the end of our path that seems like a journey through time, who protected Julius Caesar, in her temple of which today only two marvellous columns remain, re-erected, not by chance, in Napoleonic times.

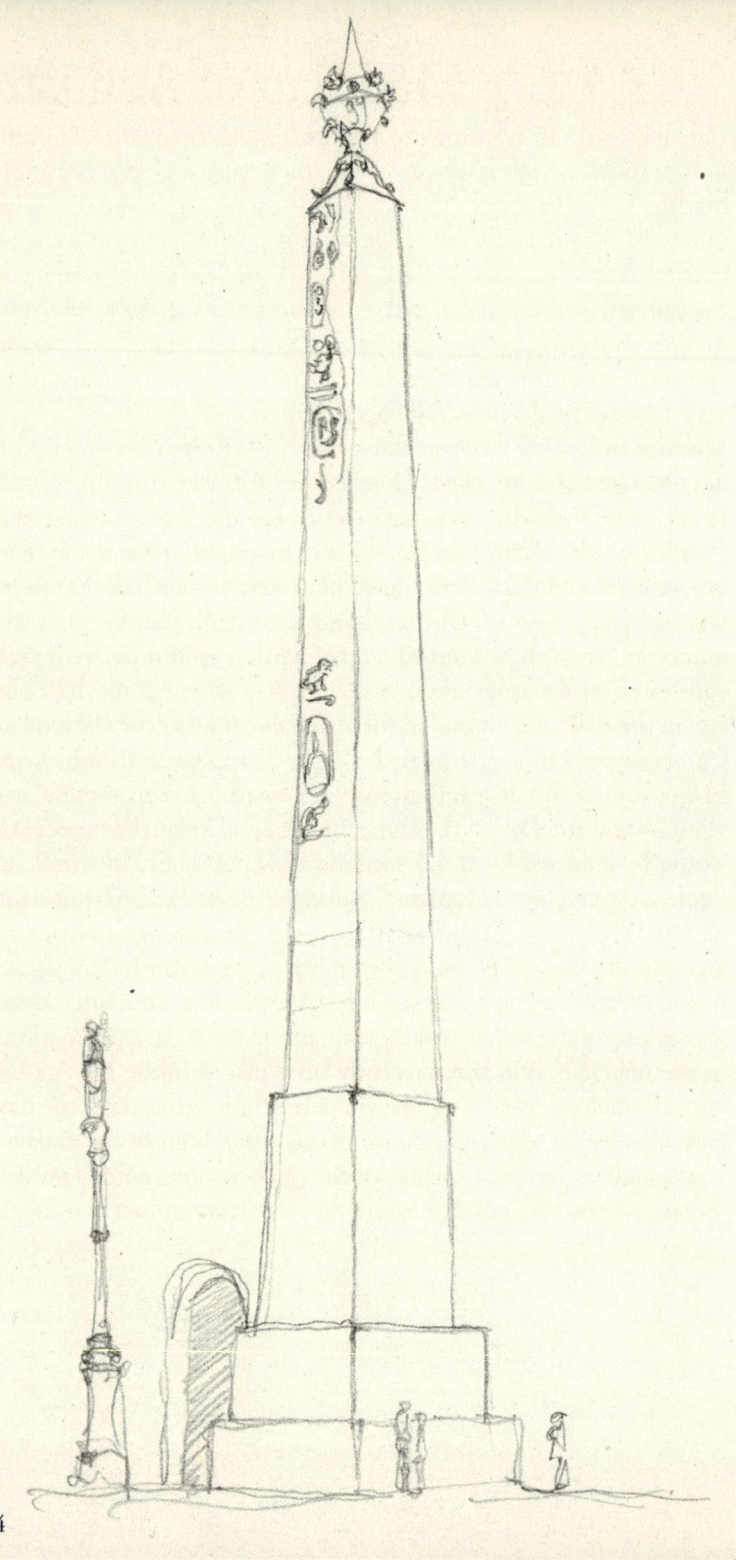

89 Meridian of Augustus
where you can discover the first public clock in Rome

For the visit
Via di Campo Marzio, 48
Although the meridian is under the care of the Soprintendenza Archeologica di Roma, permission to visit is granted by the owners of the property, the only ones who have access to the basement where you will find the site. To request a visit, call 06 33610144 or 06 33612607. Getting in touch won't be easy: they will ask you to send an e-mail and will make you wait days before you obtain permission.
In time, you will succeed.

After having imposed peace over a vanquished territory, the Emperor Augustus, from 10 B.C. onwards, turned his attention to visibly showing the might of his power in Rome too. Therefore, the famous *Pax Augusta* took the form of temples, mausoleums and extraordinary monuments. Some of them are still perfectly visible, such as the Temple to Mars Ultor, whilst others are hidden underground, accessible only to those who have the patience to follow some rather complex routes. One of these is the Meridian, the famous sundial the Emperor had made on the Field of Mars. It would have shown the hour of the day and read the annual calendar connecting the life and accomplishments of the Emperor with the movement of the sun and the planets. To understand its workings you can observe the scale model that has recently been placed inside the Ara Pacis, originally a part of this project: on the day of the Autumn equinox, Augustus' birthday, the shadow of the clock stopped exactly inside the Ara, celebrating the relation between the *Gens Julia* and the solar system. Admiring its remains in person, however, is a bit more complicated. One of the reasons for the "disappearance" of the Meridian was due to the fact that its design did not coincide with the movement of the sun along the Italian latitude: Pliny told that the mathematician, Facundus Novus, had calculated the project of the meridian from Alexandria, Egypt, without taking into consideration that the sun cast its shadow in Rome with a different inclination. On Augutus' death, sources had already ceased to speak of it. Having lost its function, the monument became a marble and bronze quarry, until it was covered with buildings in the Middle Ages and completely obscured from view. It was only in the 1960s, during the restructuring of a building in Campo Marzio, that strange traces of travertine marble with bronze inserts were found in the foundations. It was a group of Germans that started the excavations, and discovered in the building's basement, eight metres down, the only intact remnants of Augustus's celebrated clock: the central meridian with signs from the zodiac and writing in Greek. According to their reading, we would find ourselves in the month of April, under the sign of Aries, when "the winds fall", i.e. at the beginning of Spring and warmer air. Actually, a proportional calculation reveals these events taking place much earlier on the Meridian. It is still, however, an exceptional discovery that the Soprintendenza Archeologica di Roma, responsible for the care of the find, has not managed to exhibit to the public as it deserves to be. To gain access to the site, you need to pass through a private property, a building abandoned for years, a stone's throw from the Parliament. The keys to the basement are in the hands of the owners, who inexplicably have left both the building and the treasure it holds in a truly precarious state. The presence of ground water causes the marble to be constantly covered in a layer of water, making everything appear rather attractive, but just as dangerous to the longevity of the ancient materials. If you want to visit this place, arm yourself with patience and know that, it will only happen after a long series of telephone calls. Nevertheless, it truly is worth it.

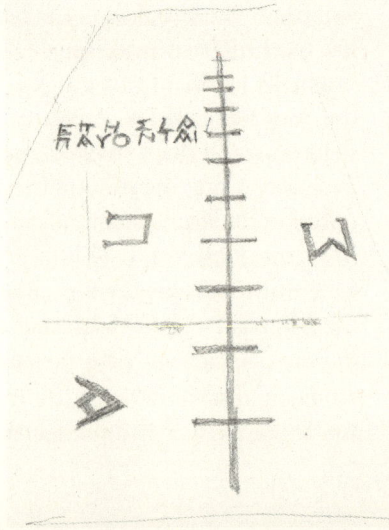

90 Hypogeum of Via Livenza
where a garage holds the Fountain of Diana

For the visit
Via Livenza, 4
Contact the booking service of the Comune di Roma by calling 060608.
Guide service available.
Entrance fee.

The thing that strikes people the most when they come to this hypogeum is that they find themselves in an underground place that has nothing at all to do with burial rites. Straight after the entrance (a structure more like an electricity junction box than an ancient monument), you descend the original steps, a sign that even in Ancient times this place was underground. A stamp with Constantine's monogram dates this place to the IV century A.D. Even the decorations date well to this period, with the passage from paganism to Christianity having created "transitional" places of worship where Christian images lived alongside Olympian ones. On one side of the room, a huge arch gives onto a basin covered in cocciopesto (hydraulic mortar). The basin is quite deep and can be accessed by some rather awkward steps: they were perhaps used for maintenance, certainly not for plunging into the basin. Water came out of the terracotta fixture, and was regulated by a system of sluice gates found on the left-hand side of the basin. The wall at the back is completely frescoed. The niche (in a decentralized position with respect to the basin) was painted to resemble marble and houses in the lunette a vase from which water is flowing and being drunk by birds. On the left, Diana appears in the act of drawing an arrow from her quiver and causing two stags to run away, whilst on the opposite side a nymph leaning on a pole caresses a fallow deer. The theme of water returns in the mosaic decorating the arch: only the feet remain of the two figures. One is on his knees drinking water flowing from a rock, the other is standing. From these small details, it has been established as a scene depicting Peter-Moses quenching a centurion's thirst with water flowing from a rock. This place was without a doubt conceived for an activity linked to water. The wildest hypotheses have been formulated to explain the many curious details, but none, as yet, has fully satisfied archaeologists. Not all the details fit together: if it were a nymphaeum, it would not be found at this depth underground; if it were a baptismal fountain, the presence of Diana would be inexplicable; if it were a swimming pool, it would have been too awkward (and why underground?) The last hypotheses tend to connect the place with a sect involved in cultish practices of the mysterious kind. Paribeni, who undertook the first excavations of the hypogeum, hypothesized, citing the presence of the basin, that it could have been a sanctuary belonging to a mystic sect founded in Greece, the *Baptes*, who venerated the Thracian goddess *Kotys*, often likened to Artemis, and practiced, during their orgy-like sacred ceremonies, ritual bathing in cold water with the aim of bringing on the shock of ecstasy. (A. Gallito)

91 Insula Romana di San Paolo alla Regola
where an Ancient Roman building is still inhabited

For the visit
Via di San Paolo alla Regola, 16
Contact the booking service of the Comune di Roma by calling 060608.
Guide service available.
Entrance fee.

It is rare to discover that the walls in a modern building are actually from the 1st century A.D. This is what happened at Palazzo Specchi, where the facade clearly shows the structure's Roman reticulated brickwork. It is the top two floors of an enormous building the origins of which date back to Flavian's rule and which has, over the centuries, never been abandoned or knocked down. Obviously, over time its function has changed.

There are three levels in the substratum, which tell you how this building came into being and how it developed in relation to the river, which also caused its soon being buried underground. The first rooms, those deepest down, have been identified as *horrea*, stock rooms, which actually extend as far as the Ministry of Justice quite a few metres distant. On the way back up to the surface, you encounter different settings with different atmospheres. The Sala della Colonna, for example, reveals the presence of an ancient courtyard, which was overlooked by several homes, indicated by the numerous filled-in windows. In the same manner, some of the black and white mosaic flooring is testimony to the fact that at a certain time these rooms were used as a home, next to which was a washhouse, which made use of the water from the river. A lovely cross-section of daily life and above all, a rare exhibition of the internal stratification of a building.

92 Cistern of the Sette Sale
where the water fed the Emperor's thermal baths

For the visit
Via delle Terme di Traiano, 5/b
Contact the booking service of the Comune di Roma calling 060608.
Guide service available.
Entrance fee.

It is already well known that the Romans were superb hydraulic engineers. What is less known is that in Imperial days each inhabitant in Rome had available to them twice as many litres of water than there are available today. Only favourable conditions like these could permit the waste of water necessary to feed monumental baths such as Trajan's on the Oppian Hill. One clear aspect of this generous use of water is visible in the cistern of Sette Sale (Seven Rooms) which was able to hold up to eight million litres of water. It was an imposing structure on two levels, which in the 4th century A.D. would be used as a base for a *domus*. The walls of the Sette Sale are covered in cocciopesto (hydraulic mortar) and the openings are orientated diagonally to each other to lessen the pressure generated by the great quantity of water and avoid currents of water. Some of the lateral openings served as access points for cleaning. The structure was only partly underground: whilst one curved wall rested directly against the hill, in order to better cope with the pressure of the water, the walls opposite made up a proper façade visible from outside and decorated in brickwork. The rapport between the two superimposed floors allowed the Cistern to have the right inclination for maintaining a constant flow of water towards the Baths. Nothing was left to chance.

93 Mithraeum of Santa Prisca
where a Church replaces the mithraic temple

For the visit
Via di Santa Prisca, 13
Visits are carried out by the archaeologists of PIERRECI CODESS the second and fourth Sunday of each month.
At 16:00 for individuals and at 15:00 and 17:00 for groups.
Book on 06 39967700.
Guide service available.
Entrance fee.

The characteristics of the mithraic rites have already been discussed in the descriptions of other sites (Mithraeum of Circus Maximus and of Palazzo Barberini), just as were the details relating to mithraic iconography. A visit to the Mithraeum at Santa Prisca is useful in terms of further reflection upon the fate of this religion, which was far more widespread than Christianity in Imperial Rome, but then suddenly disappeared. There are many similarities between the two religions: Mithras was born on the 25th December, the day of *Sol Invictus*, and one of his first miracles was to cause water to flow from a rock after having struck it with his knife. One of the traditions regarding the birth of Mithras tells of his coming from a virgin mother. The highest level in the mithraic pyramid is the *Pater Patrum*, which when abbreviated give us "Pa-Pa" (in Italian also meaning "Pope"). The final ceremony in the initiation saw the neophytes being baptized, followed by a banquet of bread and blood... bulls blood. There are many aspects that bring these two religions together, however, there is one that tends to disassociate them somewhat: Mithraism only admitted men. Women were kept outside. It would have been this choice that sealed the religion's fate and its eventual exile at the end of the 4th century A.D.. The women, excluded from Mithraism, started to commit to Christianity and bring their children up in this faith. As is known, in Ancient Rome, children were under their mothers' care until they reached puberty.

It was thus only when they reached adolescence that they had the opportunity to get close to Mithras. Too late: their faith had already been established. The new generations of Romans grew up with Christianity and put this esoteric cult aside, to be gradually forgotten forever. To erase any trace of it, many Christian communities decided to build new churches right on the foundations of the mithraea, as is the case of Santa Prisca. Under the church, after crossing the rooms of a 2nd century A.D. *domus* and the crypt frescoed in the 17th century, you reach the mithraeum, which is still made up of a few rooms. The first has been recognized as the room in which the sacrifices of small animals took place, in remembrance of the killing of the bull by Mithras. The Aula dell'Agape (feast room) is introduced by two niches where the statues of *Cautes* and *Cautopates* were displayed (only the former remains), beyond which the "triclinium" opens up. On the walls, two processions illustrate the seven stages of mithraic initiation on one side and, on the other, a procession of followers bringing gifts to the *Pater Patrum*. In the tauroctony in relief the figure of Oceanus appears, which possibly used to pour water into a basin below.

From here, you pass through two other rooms, a sort of sacristy and the initiation room. We do not know what these initiation rites consisted of, probably trials of resistance where the neophytes would have to show self-control, maybe by immersing himself in a bath of freezing water or drinking the bull's blood.

94 Excubitorium of the VII Cohort
where you can read the fire fighters' graffiti

For the visit
*Via della Settima Coorte, 9
(Viale Trastevere)*
Contact the booking service at the Comune di Roma by calling 060608.
Guide service available.
Entrance fee.

The Emperor Augustus really thought of even the most minute detail in order to render real and enduring the *Pax* that bore his name. He did not think only of extending and consolidating the borders of the Empire, he above all thought of organizing the life of Rome, a city in expansion, enriched with important monuments for propaganda. He divided Rome into 14 zones and entrusted their security to 7 well-trained forces of order. In particular, he created a regiment specialized in putting out fires, which were a frequent occurrence in a city predominantly made of wood. These soldiers also had the job of carrying out nightly rounds, to control fights, assassins and pyromaniacs. Each cohort could count on a barracks in one zone and a detachment in the other. It was this latter guard post that became known as the *Excubitorium*. In the 19th century, one was discovered at eight metres depth in the heart of Trastevere, a zone which even at that time was particularly at risk as it was already densely populated, mostly by foreigners. The work the firefighters did was often recounted in the graffiti left on the walls of the room, where one wrote: «I'm tired, change the guard!». More often though the phrases are wishing luck to the Emperor or thanking their gods for ending the night shift (*sebaciaria*).

Most of the writings have, with time, been eradicated, but at the time of their discovery, they were all copied down into a document that still exists today. Inside, the structure is organized into rooms useful for everyday life: an altar conserved the image of the *Genius excubitori*, the divinity protecting firefighters, which still shows some signs of painting. Going underground, you enter into a "kitchen", where a *dolium* (jar) dug out of the earth was used to conserve oil, wheat and wine. A little further on, we have the toilet and small rooms for resting, where the soldiers must have spent many boring hours, given the tone of the messages they left for posterity.

95 Necropolis of the Vatican and of Via Triumphalis
where you can find the tomb of Peter

For the visit
Piazza San Pietro (excavation entrance)
The visit needs to be booked at least twenty days in advance by sending a fax to 06 69885518 or an e-mail to: visitedidattiche.musei@scv.va. In the request specify the day, the number of visitors and the language spoken. Guide service available.
Entrance fee.

The Vatican "hill" owes its fortune to the presence of numerous necropoles. In one of these, in the 1st century A.D., the Apostle Peter was buried and over the centuries, his presence has transformed a normal cemetery into the main destination for pilgrims in the Christian world. It is not easy getting your bearings at nine metres down under St. Peter's Basilica. The first archaeological remains date back to the 2nd century A.D. and go up to the 4th century A.D., distributed in small, splendid sepulchres, where it is possible to read the entire Roman funeral repertoire. The Pontifical Commission for Sacred Archaeology has identified two different necropoles: one of these hosts the Tomb of Peter. The other was only discovered in 2003, during work being carried out on the construction of a parking lot in the Vatican City. The latter can be found on the road that leads to Veio, known as *Via Triumphalis*. In the first cemetery, you can see how, from the 2nd century A.D., the sepulchres point towards a precise point: the place identified as the Tomb of Peter. The deceased would have asked to be buried close to the Saint or at least within sight of the tomb. The route includes many tombs with elegant decorations, often covered or disturbed by the foundations of the Constantine-era basilica and by other structures that hold up the

Renaissance basilica. Crossing the park between pilasters holding up Bernini's canopy and medieval walls, it is hard to imagine that it used to be open to the elements. When Constantine decided to use the area for the construction of the Basilica and organize a pilgrimage which was already going to be massive, the workers were wise enough not to destroy all the sepulchres. At times, they left some of the tombs accessible to family members of the deceased or else they were worried that the work could cause damage to the sarcophagi. It is for this reason that sometimes the route for the visit follows a displacement thought up centuries ago. Overall, in two necropoles, forty sepulchral edifices have been brought to light, some decorated with frescoes, stuccoes and floor mosaics. There are, furthermore, over two hundred tombs identified with gravestones, altars and inscriptions, which often give the birth place and occupation of the deceased.

96 Colombarium of Vigna Codini
where the ashes of a court jester are kept

For the visit
Via di Porta San Sebastiano, 13
The site is found on a private property.
Visits take place on a Wednesday and Thursday morning upon prior booking which can be obtained sending a fax to 06 48900740.
No more than 15 people can enter at a time. In the request, include a list of all the participants' names.
Own guide.
Free entrance.

Whoever has a villa on Appia Antica has to expect that in the earth beneath some truly authentic treasures are hidden. The old Codini Vineyards hide a cooperative sepulchre built in the 1st century A.D., for the most part financed by freemen of the Imperial Court who wanted to guarantee themselves a worthy burial place. What is particular about this place is the fact that it is made up of three different columbaria, belonging to different eras and social classes. The first of these held the ashes of a jester to Tiberius' court and a tax collector from Lyon, the second is occupied, at the centre, by a table that used to hold three great urns, the third, perhaps the most unusual, is the one that was destined for people with the largest disposable incomes. It has been shaped into a U, and houses rectangular niches and some arcosolia, proof that the use of this sepulchre lasted for centuries. Proof of the wealth of this columbarium is the use of travertine marble. In some points you can still see the shelves used to hold the wooden beams that allowed people to reach the higher niches. The inscriptions, richer than usual, are worth particular attention. Not only do they give the name of the deceased, but also admonitions and prayers. Perhaps the most explicit one warns: «Do not touch, oh mortal, hands respect the Gods!», a warning to the frequent grave-robbers to be on guard stealing the precious urns.

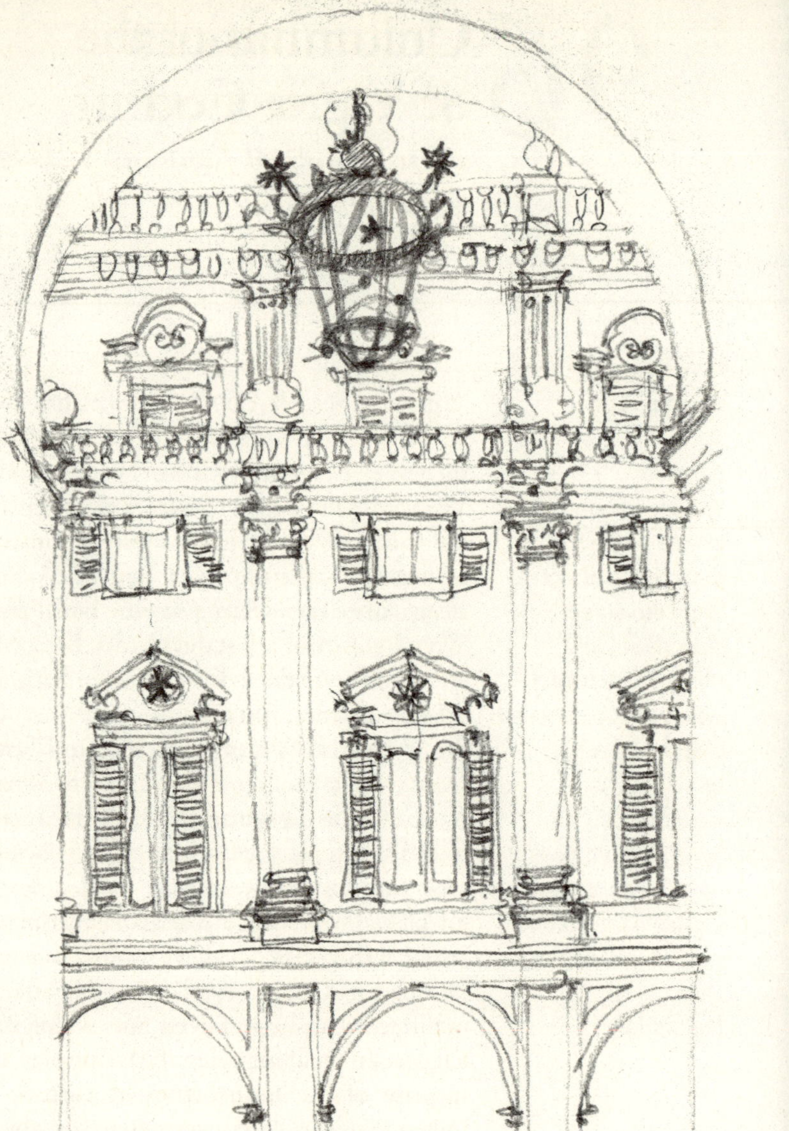

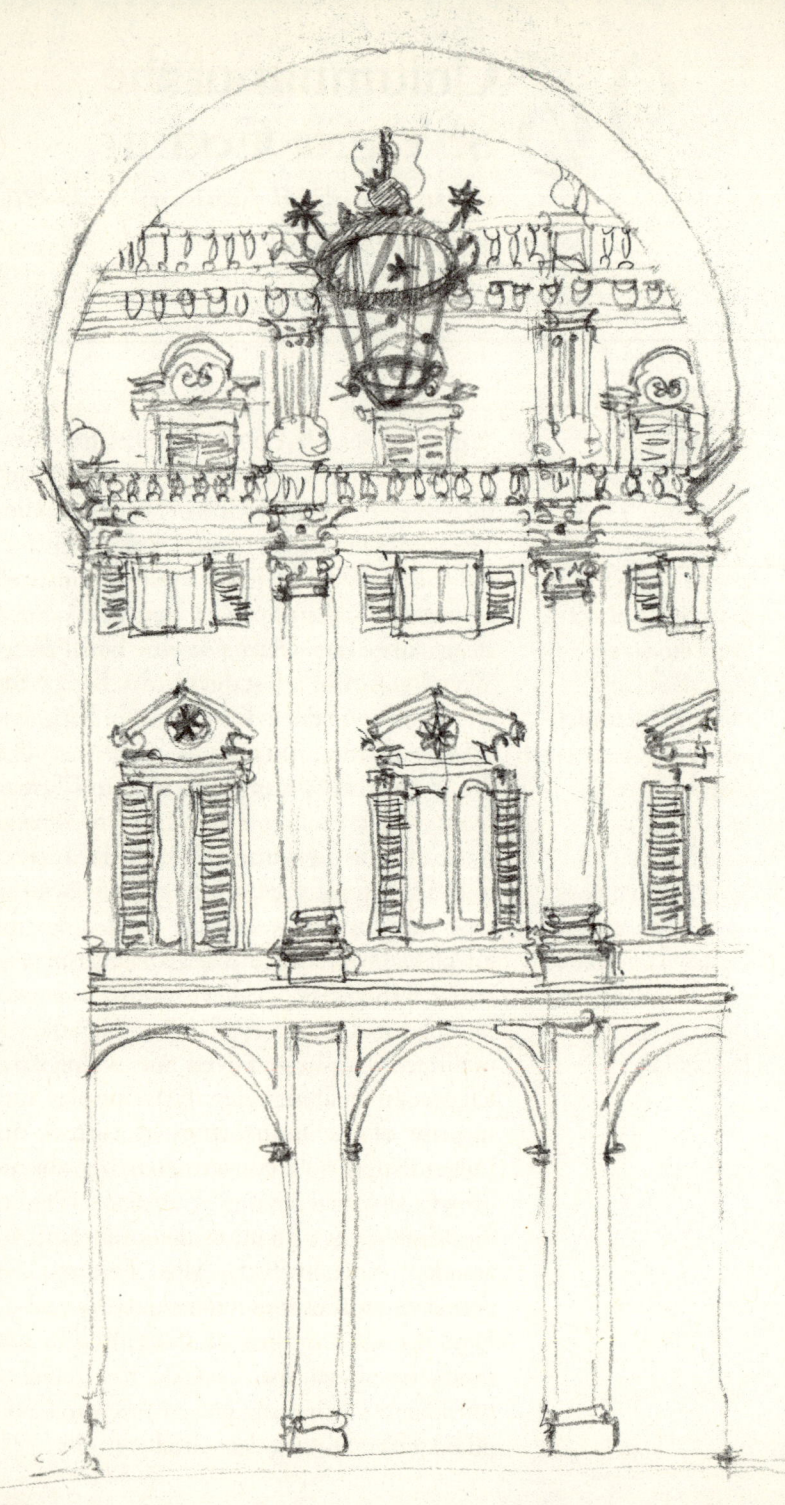

97 Oratorium of the Seven Sleepers

where an ancient fresco can be found in a cellar

For the visit
Via di Porta San Sebastiano, 7
The site is located on a private property.
To book a visit send a fax to 06 4742615 or an e-mail to:
aurorapallavicini@saita.it.
Own guide.
Free entrance.

Exploring the most hidden places in Rome often offers the chance to get to know the lesser-known legends. One of these concerns the Sette Dormienti (Seven Sleepers) from Ephesus. During the persecutions carried out by Emperor Decius (mid-3rd century A.D.) a group of seven youths from Asia Minor refused to worship the pagan gods. They were put in prison and then released. To aviod being re-arrested, they hid in a grotto under the Caélian Hill, from which one of them came out every day to replenish stocks. Discovered by the guards, they were bricked into the cave alive. Waiting for their deaths, they fell asleep. They were woken up by bricklayers who were working on constructing a fold. Only then did they realize that two centuries had passed by and that Christianity was now a freely practiced and widespread religion. In their tale hides the waiting for and surprise of the resurrection of corpses on Judgement Day, a concern that has always been wide-spread amongst Christians, who, in the Middle Ages, began to dedicate places of worship to the Seven Sleepers. This was the period when all stories referring to the End of Days acquired a supreme value, due to the rampant pessimism caused by frequent proclamations that the end of the world was nigh. The Oratory was built in the 12th

century inside a structure from Roman times, ruins of a multi-levelled Roman house. It was abandoned many times due to its being rather far from the city centre; first in the 14th century, then, despite the restorations carried out by Pope Clement XI, in 1710, it was transformed into a storage area for the farmhouse which, in the meantime, had risen on the upper floors. The structure is still inhabited today. The ground floor (slightly at basement level) houses the fascinating frescoes recounted by Armellini, who discovered them in 1875. «It is an oratory dedicated to Archangel Gabriel, a golden figure of whom remains in the niche at the back with his arms wide open, and under the image is his name: Gabriel». It is truly deplorable that a distinguished monument to the history of worship and the paintings that still adorn the walls, lies abandoned and reduced to being used as a countryside cellar and rubbish tip. The pictures represent, in the upper lunette of the far wall, the bust of the Saviour amongst a chorus of adoring angels. In the corners of the lunette remain the portraits of the two people who commissioned the painting and who are today attributed with the paintings in the underground basilica of St. Clement. They are the married couple, Beno de Rapiza and Maria, who lived between the 12th and 13th centuries, the era to which the paintings belong; in fact beneath the images you can see the names Beno and Maria. Many figures of angels, saintly Greek monks and belted monks with halos on their heads adorn the side walls of this oratory, which I discovered about 11 years ago». Today it can be found in a good state of preservation, thanks to the private owners who own the entire structure and the surrounding park.

98 Temple of Via delle Botteghe Oscure
where the free wheat was distributed

For the visit
Via Celsa, 3
Contact the booking service of the Comune di Roma by calling 060608.
Guide service available.
Entrance fee.

They are among the liveliest figures from ancient mythology. They are always present by the side of each divinity and often unleash unstoppable passion in the most important of gods. We are talking about the nymphs, who have passed into history as young virgins with a gracious and provocative appearance. They live for the most part in the woods, near springs, and help humans, above all if they are particularly attractive. Despite not having any supernatural powers, in Rome, they were deemed worthy of their own temple. This place had assumed a noteworthy role of importance for the city already in the Republican era, as it was directly under its portico that the periodic distribution of wheat to the less wealthy took place. We are halfway between the Area Sacra of Largo Argentina and via delle Botteghe Oscure: here a long series of arches used to connect the *Porticus Minucia Vetus* to the *Porticus Minucia Frumentaria*. The first was built in 107 B.C. by Marcus Minucius Rufus, a descendant of Minucius Augurinus after whom the Colonna Minicia was named, following his triumph over the Scordisci (an ancient people from Thrace). The second is nothing more than a double of the *Vetus*, probably erected under the reign of Claudius (first half of the 1st century A.D.). In that time, the *porticus* also included the Temple of the

Nymphs, on today's via delle Botteghe Oscure, and became the administrative centre for the control and effective distribution of grain to the people. Today, you can still see standing some of the columns from the Temple's *pronaos*, included amongst the city's most visited spots. At the foot of the columns are some rooms where you can see fragments of marble and the parts of the Temple where the lists were kept detailing who had the right to a ration of wheat. It was a place of great importance for the best part of the population of Rome. This practice, already in place in the 1st century B.C. and developed further under the Empire, shows that the Romans were not alien to the concept of welfare.

A GYMNASIUM

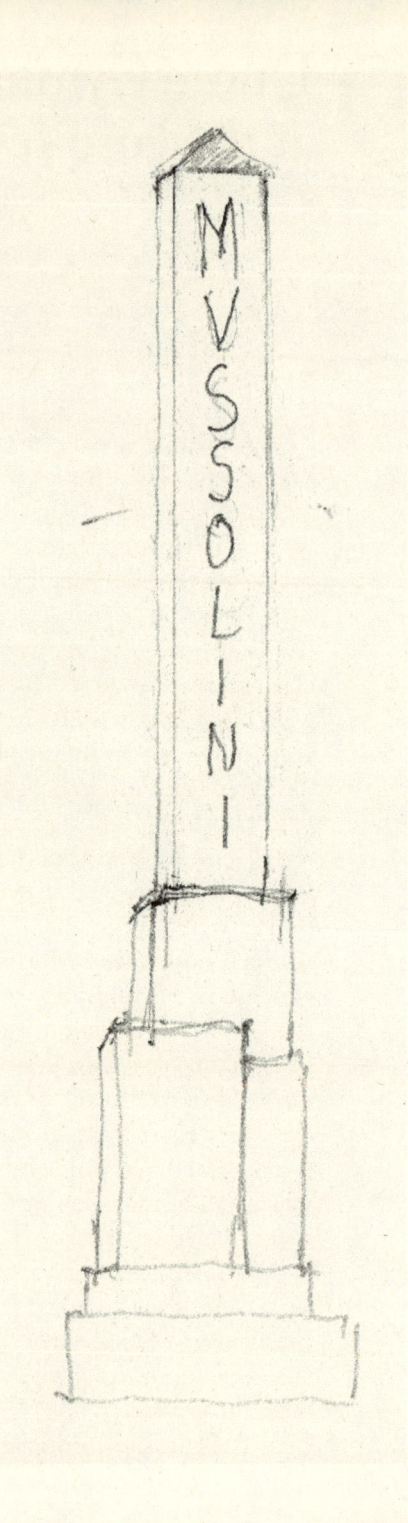

99 Duce's Gymnasium at the Foro Italico
where Mussolini used to go tanning

For the visit
Foro Italico complex
Requests for a visit need to be made on the headed paper of a cultural association and sent by fax to 06 36857199.
In the request propose a couple of dates and include a mobile phone number to be contacted on.
For further information call 06 36857743.
Guide service available.
Free entrance.

«The room is conceived to be bare and bright, of a Greek purity, so as to exalt each active gesture and movement. Such essentiality in the plastic treatment of the surfaces brings out the Hall's depths of spatial and linear harmony, rendered even more sensitive by the lively beats of light, magically reflected by clean marble walls». This was how Luigi Moretti, celebrated architect of the twenty years of Fascism in Italy, described the Gymnasium of the Foro Italico, as often happened with buildings from that time. In this room too, every minute detail has been planned, from the flooring and the cut of the marbles on the walls to the inlaid decoration of the wooden doors. Mussolini never spared any expense in his building works (just look at the EUR), so you can imagine that the gym intended for his own personal training was no exception. Already at the entrance, you tread on a mosaic carpet with an abstract design by Gino Severini, whilst inside the hall, which still contains some exercise equipment, is dominated by a bronze statue of the *Athlete* by Silvio Canevari. But, perhaps the most surprising details are the partitions covered in marble, which separate the Gym from the changing room and from the continuous spiral staircase, which takes you up to the top floor dedicated to "artificial sun" treatment.

If you want to get more information please check the website

www.99secretplaces.com

or write to

info@99secretplaces.com

CULTURAL ASSOCIATIONS

The following list in alphabetical order includes some of the biggest cultural associations which organize guided visits to some of the 99 secret places named in this book. The list is not intended to be exhaustive, but to give an idea of the organizations that can be contacted for special access.

ALTAIR
Tel. 068100805
www.associazionealtair.it

ARCHEODOMANI
Tel. 0665744547
www.archeodomani.com

ARCHIMEDE
Tel. 3392201463
       3398616632

ARCIMBOLDO
Tel.: 0670475449
arcimboldo_it@hotmail.com

L'ARTEFICIO
Tel. 0696843848
www.larteficio.it

CITTÀ NASCOSTA
Tel. 063216059
www.cittanascosta.com

EOS
Tel. 0686907230 - 3496732734
www.eoscultura.it

FAI
Tel. 066879376
www.fondoambiente.it

FLUMEN
Tel. 0670493877
www.flumen.it

GENIUS LOCI
Tel. 0635058050
www.geniuslociroma.org

ITINERA
Tel 0627800785
www.itinera.biz

NINE
Tel. 3314565902
www.associazionenine.it

M'ARTE
Tel. 3921637469
www.associazionemarte.org

OBELISCO
Tel. 3476753799
www.associazioneobelisco.com

PALLADIO
Tel. 066867897
www.associazionepalladio.com

RAFFAELLO SANZIO
Tel. 3478257353
assoc.raffaellosanzio@gmail.com

RES ANTIQUAE
Tel. 0687905747 - 3478249859
www.resantiquae.it

ROMA SOTTERRANEA
Tel. 0654221988
www.romasotterranea.com

Romana Voli d'Arte
Tel. 3477518797
www.volidarte.com

Il Salotto delle Arti
Tel. 0635500984
www.ilsalottodellearti.it

Severiana
Tel. 3405708124
www.severiana.it

Sotterranei di Roma
Tel. 3473811874
www.sotterraneidiroma.it

Trasecoli
Tel. 3452899851
www.trasecoli.it

INDEX OF PLACES IN ORDER OF APPEARANCE

1	Palazzo Colonna	9
2	Casino Ludovisi	11
3	Villa Albani	15
4	Palazzo Farnese	17
5	Palazzo Pamphilj	21
6	Palazzo Sacchetti	25
7	Palazzo dei Penitenzieri	29
8	Palazzo Falconieri	33
9	Palazzo della Cancelleria	35
10	Aurora Pallavicini's Casino	39
11	The Apartment of the Council of State at Palazzo Spada	41
12	Palazzo Patrizi	43
13	Palazzo Salviati	45
14	Casino del Bel Respiro	47
15	Palazzo Rondinini	51
16	Palazzo Antici Mattei di Giove	53
17	Palazzo Chigi	55
18	Villa Madama	57
19	Palazzo Baldassini	61
20	Villa Lante	63
21	Villa Barberini	67
22	Villino Gamberini	69
23	Villino Ximenes	71
24	Palazzo della Marina	73
25	Casino di Villa Carpegna	75
26	Palazzo Montecitorio	77
27	Villa Paolina	79
28	Villino Douhet	81
29	Villa Aurelia	83
30	Palazzo Madama	85
31	Istituto Nazionale di Studi Romani	87
32	Casa dei Cavalieri di Rodi	89
33	Vatican Gardens	93
34	Casino Borghese	95
35	Palazzo della Consulta	97
36	Casina of Cardinal Bessarione	99
37	Villino Huffer	103
38	Palazzo Koch	105

39	Palazzo Vidoni Caffarelli	107
40	Convent of Trinità dei Monti	111
41	Monastero delle Oblate a Tor de' Specchi	115
42	Antica Spezieria di Santa Maria della Scala	117
43	Vatican Secret Archives and Torre dei Venti	119
44	Biblioteca Angelica	121
45	Insula sapientiae	123
46	Collegio di Santa Maria dell'Umiltà	125
47	San Giovanni Decollato	127
48	Saints Luca and Martina	129
49	Sistine Chapel	131
50	Chapel of the Re Magi	133
51	Santa Maria del Priorato	135
52	San Giovanni in Oleo	137
53	San Giovanni Calibita	139
54	San Giuliano of the Flemings	141
55	San Girolamo della Carità	143
56	Sant'Urbano alla Caffarella	145
57	San Nicola dei Lorenesi	147
58	San Giovanni Battista dei Genovesi	149
59	Sant'Eligio degli Orefici	151
60	Santa Caterina de' Funari	153
61	Santa Maria dei Sette Dolori	155
62	Convent of Santa Sabina	157
63	Underground site of Ospedale San Giovanni	161
64	Gardens of Sallust	163
65	Underground site of Santa Maria Maggiore	165
66	Mithraeum of Palazzo Barberini	167
67	Mithraeum of Circus Maximus	169
68	Necropolis of Via Ostiense	171
69	Jewish Catacombs of Vigna Randanini	173
70	Monte Testaccio	175
71	Lucio Peto's Mausoleum	177
72	Hypogeum of Trebio Giusto	179
73	Hypogeum of the Aureli	181
74	Basilica and Catacombs of Generosa	183
75	Acquedotto Vergine	185
76	Tempio Rotondo	187
77	Pyramid of Caio Cestio	189
78	Jewish Catacombs of Villa Torlonia	191
79	Tombs of Via Latina	193

80	Basilica and Catacombs of San Valentino	195
81	Hypogeum of Via Dino Compagni	197
82	Cloaca Maxima	199
83	Syriac Sanctuary	201
84	Necropolis of Villa Pamphilj	203
85	Columbarium of Pomponio Hylas	205
86	Mausoleum of Monte del Grano	207
87	Mausoleum of Sant'Elena	209
88	Imperial Forum	211
89	Meridian of Augustus	215
90	Hypogeum of Via Livenza	217
91	Insula Romana di San Paolo alla Regola	219
92	Cistern of the Sette Sale	221
93	Mithraeum of Santa Prisca	223
94	Excubitorium of the VII Cohort	225
95	Necropolis of the Vatican and of Via Triumphalis	227
96	Columbarium of Vigna Codini	229
97	Oratory of the Seven Sleepers	231
98	Temple of Via delle Botteghe Oscure	233
99	Duce's Gymnasium at the Foro Italico	235

INDEX OF PLACES IN ALPHABETICAL ORDER

75	Acquedotto Vergine	185
10	Aurora Pallavicini's Casino	39
42	Antica Spezieria di Santa Maria della Scala	117
80	Basilica and Catacombs of San Valentino	195
74	Basilica and Catacombs of Generosa	183
44	Biblioteca Angelica	121
50	Chapel of the Re Magi	133
62	Convent and Underground site of Santa Sabina	157
32	Casa dei Cavalieri di Rodi	89
36	Casina of Cardinal Bessarione	99
34	Casino Borghese	95
14	Casino del Bel Respiro	47
25	Casino di Villa Carpegna	75
2	Casino Ludovisi	11
92	Cistern of the Sette Sale	221
82	Cloaca Maxima	199
46	Collegio di S.Maria dell'Umiltà	125
96	Colombarium of Vigna Codini	229
85	Colombarium of Pomponio Hylas	205
40	Convent of Trinità dei Monti	111
99	Duce's Gymnasium at the Foro Italico	237
94	Excubitorium of the VII Cohort	225
64	Gardens of Sallust	163
73	Hypogeum of the Aureli	181
72	Hypogeum of Trebio Giusto	179
81	Hypogeum of Via Dino Compagni	197
90	Hypogeum of Via Livenza	217
91	Insula Romana di San Paolo alla Regola	219
45	Insula sapientiae	123
88	Imperial Forum	211
31	Istituto Nazionale di Studi Romani	87
78	Jewish Catacombs of Villa Torlonia	191
69	Jewish Catacombs of Vigna Randanini	173
71	Lucio Peto's Mausoleum	177
86	Mausoleum of Monte del Grano	207
87	Mausoleum of Sant'Elena	209
89	Meridian of Augustus	215
67	Mithraeum of Circus Maximus	169

66	Mithraeum of Palazzo Barberini	167
93	Mithraeum of Santa Prisca	223
41	Monastero delle Oblate a Tor de' Specchi	115
70	Monte Testaccio	175
68	Necropolis of Via Ostiense	171
84	Necropolis of Villa Pamphilj	203
95	Necropolis of the Vatican and of Via Triumphalis	227
97	Oratory of the Seven Sleepers	231
16	Palazzo Antici Mattei di Giove	53
19	Palazzo Baldassini	61
17	Palazzo Chigi	55
1	Palazzo Colonna	9
7	Palazzo dei Penitenzieri	29
9	Palazzo della Cancelleria	35
35	Palazzo della Consulta	97
24	Palazzo della Marina	73
8	Palazzo Falconieri	33
4	Palazzo Farnese	17
38	Palazzo Koch	105
30	Palazzo Madama	85
26	Palazzo Montecitorio	77
5	Palazzo Pamphilj	21
12	Palazzo Patrizi	43
15	Palazzo Rondinini	51
6	Palazzo Sacchetti	25
13	Palazzo Salviati	45
11	Palazzo Spada (Council of State)	41
39	Palazzo Vidoni Caffarelli	107
77	Pyramid of Caio Cestio	189
58	San Giovanni Battista dei Genovesi	149
53	San Giovanni Calibita	139
47	San Giovanni Decollato	127
52	San Giovanni in Oleo	137
55	San Girolamo della Carità	143
54	San Giuliano of the Flemings	141
57	San Nicola dei Lorenesi	147
59	Sant'Eligio degli Orefici	151
56	Sant'Urbano alla Caffarella	145
60	Santa Caterina de' Funari	153
61	Santa Maria dei Sette Dolori	155
51	Santa Maria del Priorato	135

48	Saints Luca and Martina	129
43	Vatican Secret Archives and Torre dei Venti	119
83	Syriac Sanctuary	201
49	Sistine Chapel	131
98	Temple of Via delle Botteghe Oscure	233
76	Tempio Rotondo	187
79	Tombs of Via Latina	193
63	Underground site of Ospedale San Giovanni	161
65	Underground site of Santa Maria Maggiore	165
33	Vatican Gardens	93
3	Villa Albani	15
29	Villa Aurelia	83
21	Villa Barberini	67
20	Villa Lante	63
18	Villa Madama	57
27	Villa Paolina	79
28	Villino Douhet	81
22	Villino Gamberini	69
37	Villino Hüffer	103
23	Villino Ximenes	71

INDEX OF PLACES BY AREA

The names of the areas are merely indicative. They highlight the most famous sights near the place or area of the city.

APPIA ANTICA

36	Casina of Cardinal Bessarione	99
52	San Giovanni in Oleo	137
56	Sant'Urbano alla Caffarella	145
69	Jewish Catacombs of Vigna Randanini	173
79	Tombs of Via Latina	193
85	Colombarium of Pomponio Hylas	205
96	Colombarium of Vigna Codini	229
97	Oratory of the Seven Sleepers	231

AVENTINE

31	Istituto Nazionale di Studi Romani	87
51	Santa Maria del Priorato	135
62	Convent and Underground site of Santa Sabina	157
93	Mithraeum of Santa Prisca	223

ESQUILINE

65	Underground site of Santa Maria Maggiore	165
73	Hypogeum of the Aureli	181

PIAZZA DEL POPOLO

15	Palazzo Rondinini	51
24	Palazzo della Marina	73
40	Convent of Trinità dei Monti	111

PIAZZA NAVONA

4	Palazzo Farnese	17
5	Palazzo Pamphilj	21
6	Palazzo Sacchetti	25
8	Palazzo Falconieri	33

9	Palazzo della Cancelleria	35
11	Apartment of the Council of State at Palazzo Spada	41
12	Palazzo Patrizi	43
19	Palazzo Baldassini	61
26	Palazzo Montecitorio	77
30	Palazzo Madama	85
35	Palazzo della Consulta	97
39	Palazzo Vidoni Caffarelli	107
44	Biblioteca Angelica	121
45	Insula sapientiae	123
55	San Girolamo della Carità	143
57	San Nicola dei Lorenesi	147
59	Sant'Eligio degli Orefici	151
89	Meridian of Augustus	215
91	Insula Romana di San Paolo alla Regola	219

PIAZZA VENEZIA

1	Palazzo Colonna	9
10	Aurora Pallavicini's Casino	39
16	Palazzo Antici Mattei di Giove	53
17	Palazzo Chigi	55
32	Casa dei Cavalieri di Rodi	89
37	Villino Huffer	103
38	Palazzo Koch	105
41	Monastero delle Oblate a Tor de' Specchi	115
46	Collegio di Santa Maria dell'Umiltà	125
47	San Giovanni Decollato	127
48	Saints Luca and Martina	129
50	Cappella dei Re Magi	133
54	San Giuliano of the Flemings	141
60	Santa Caterina de' Funari	153
66	Mithraeum of Palazzo Barberini	167
67	Mithraeum of Circus Maximus	169
75	Acquedotto Vergine	185
76	Tempio Rotondo	187
82	Cloaca Maxima	199
88	Imperial Forum	211
92	Cistern of the Sette Sale	221
98	Temple of Via delle Botteghe Oscure	233

ROMA EST

63	Underground site of Ospedale San Giovanni	161
72	Hypogeum of Trebio Giusto	179
81	Hypogeum of Via Dino Compagni	197
86	Mausoleum of Monte del Grano	207
87	Mausoleum of Sant'Elena	209

ROMA NORD

2	Casino Ludovisi	11
3	Villa Albani	15
18	Villa Madama	57
✓34	Casino Borghese	95
71	Lucio Peto's Mausoleum	177
80	Basilica and Catacombs of San Valentino	195
99	Duce's Gymnasium at the Foro Italico	237

ROMA OVEST

14	Casino del Bel Respiro	47
25	Casino di Villa Carpegna	75
68	Necropolis of Via Ostiense	171
70	Monte Testaccio	175
74	Basilica and Catacombs of Generosa	183
77	Pyramid of Caio Cestio	189
84	Necropolis of Villa Pamphilj	201

SALARIO

22	Villino Gamberini	69
23	Villino Ximenes	71
27	Villa Paolina	79
64	Gardens of Sallust	163
78	Jewish Catacombs of Villa Torlonia	191
90	Hypogeum of Via Livenza	217

TRASTEVERE

42	Antica Spezieria di Santa Maria della Scala	117
53	San Giovanni Calibita	139

58	San Giovanni Battista dei Genovesi	149
61	Santa Maria dei Sette Dolori	155
83	Syriac Sanctuary	201
94	Excubitorium of the VII Cohort	225

VATICAN

7	Palazzo dei Penitenzieri	29
13	Palazzo Salviati	45
20	Villa Lante	63
21	Villa Barberini	67
28	Villino Douhet	81
29	Villa Aurelia	83
33	Vatican Gardens	93
43	Vatican Secret Archives and Torre dei Venti	119
49	Sistine Chapel	131
95	Necropolis of the Vatican and of Via Triumphalis	227

Printing finished
May 2017

Diano Libri Srl
Modena